CW01091329

BY PAUL WALLIS

**Scripture
Union**

This book is dedicated, of course, to God.

But also to you the reader, and to all the children who will become Desert Detectives for a week under your guidance and care.

It would not have been possible to write **DESERT DETECTIVES** without the patience and support of my wife, Sylvia, and the guidance of my editor and friend, Ro. And thanks are due, too, to all the members of Croxley Green and Sarratt Baptist Church,

who piloted **Desert Detectives** and helped to develop and clarify many of the ideas in this book.

I hope you have as much fun with **Desert Detectives** as we did.

Paul Wallis April 2001

Scripture Union, 207–209 Queensway, Bletchley, Milton Keynes MK2 2EB, England.

© Paul Wallis, 2001.

ISBN 1 85999 498 9

British Library Cataloguing-in-Publication Data
A catalogue record for this book is available from the British Library.

Cover illustration by Colin Smithson
Cover design by FourNineZero
Internal design by FourNineZero
Expedition sheet artwork by Eira Reeves

Scripture quotations taken from the Contemporary English Version © American Bible Society, 1991, 1992, 1995. Anglicisations © British and Foreign Bible Society 1996. Published in the UK by HarperCollins*Publishers* and used with permission.

Printed and bound by Interprint Ltd, Malta

Scripture Union ✑

We are an international Christian charity working with churches in more than 130 countries providing resources to bring the good news about Jesus Christ to children, young people and families – and to encourage them to develop spiritually through the Bible and prayer.

As well as our network of volunteers, staff and associates who run holidays, church-based events and school Christian groups, we produce a wide range of publications and support those who use our resources through training programmes.

Visit the **Desert Detectives** website and discover additional resources and advice. Visit **www.scriptureunion.org.uk/desertdetectives**.

CONTENTS

INTRODUCTION

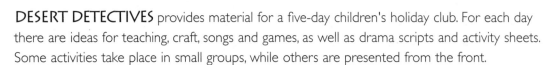

DEEP IN THE DRY DUSTY DESERT, THE DARING
DESERT DETECTIVES DILIGENTLY DIG...

DESERT DETECTIVES provides material for a five-day children's holiday club. For each day there are ideas for teaching, craft, songs and games, as well as drama scripts and activity sheets. Some activities take place in small groups, while others are presented from the front.

DESERT DETECTIVES also includes material for two Sunday services – one to launch the holiday club, and one to round it off. A service before the week is a great way to introduce the theme to your church, and encourage them to pray for the week ahead. Hopefully it will also inspire the congregation to interact with the Bible themselves! A service at the end helps to wrap up the week, and gives a chance to present the gospel to the children's parents. The material for both these services could be used to expand the full programme to seven days.

The DESERT DETECTIVES VIDEO is also available to augment the programme. The DESERT DETECTIVES' NOTEBOOK helps the children to engage with the Bible themselves.

THIS BOOK
IS DIVIDED
INTO FIVE
SECTIONS:

PART 1 What is Desert Detectives?

This tells you all about Desert Detectives – how it works, what it includes, and details about the theme and setting.

PART 2 Setting up a holiday club

Planning Desert Detectives, including legal issues and other things to consider.

PART 3 Who does what – key tasks

Putting Desert Detectives into practice. This includes the different tasks involved in Desert Detectives, shortly before the holiday club and during it too. This is also where you'll find resources and ideas for the activities that happen throughout the week, including the Desert Detectives song, drama, teaching scripts and craft ideas.

PART 4 Desert Detectives day by day

Each day described in detail.

PART 5 Other ways to use Desert Detectives

Ideas for follow-up and for using Desert Detectives with other age groups, including adults.

The back cover also has details of resources you can order, including publicity materials.

PART 1

What is **Desert Detectives?**

The aims of **Desert Detectives**

Desert Detectives is based on the Bible. Not just a few Bible stories, the whole Bible! **Desert Detectives** looks at how God's plan for the world has been worked out right through history.

Desert Detectives will help you to:
- show children that the Bible is full of exciting stories which fit together into one big story
- explain the different types of books the Bible contains (Law, History, Poetry, Prophecy, Gospels, Letters)
- introduce children to Jesus and help them discover what it means to have a relationship with him.

Desert Detectives encourages children to dig into the Bible for themselves, rather than passively expecting other people to tell them about it. Of course, the Bible is not just a great book. Its whole purpose is to tell us about our relationship with God, and our salvation through Jesus Christ. So as well as looking at the 'big picture', **Desert Detectives** focuses on certain stories in order to teach specific things about God.

THEME AND SETTING

Desert Detectives, as the name suggests, is set in a desert. Sand, palm trees, a tent, spades, picks, snakes and scorpions all help to set the scene. The **Desert Detectives** in the drama are Doug (dug), Sandy and June (dune), and they are digging for buried treasure. They've heard rumours of an ancient and powerful treasure buried somewhere in the desert. It's called the Mighty GodSword, and it's said to be very valuable. All the children become **Desert Detectives** with them.

During their search for the Mighty GodSword the **Desert Detectives** suffer a variety of mishaps, but each day they manage to dig up something interesting to send to their boss, the Professor. Each find leads the Professor to a particular Bible story. Further research then reveals how that story fits into the overall Bible story, with its different types of writing.

Summarising the whole Bible in a week is a mammoth task! But **Desert Detectives** provides the resources to help you. If you want to have a 'live' Professor, a full script is provided for each day (see pages 33 to 46), together with suggestions for illustrations and tips on making a Bible bookcase. Alternatively, the Professor features in the *DESERT DETECTIVES VIDEO*.

THE DESERT DETECTIVES VIDEO

The *DESERT DETECTIVES VIDEO* follows on from the drama each day. In each of the five episodes, the Professor receives an artefact from the **Desert Detectives**. Assisted by Famulus, he sends the intrepid explorer, Rhona Black, on five expeditions back in time, to discover a Bible story set in its context.

Of course, even though the *DESERT DETECTIVES VIDEO* is strongly integrated with the rest of the **DESERT DETECTIVES** programme, it will stand on its own. It will therefore continue to be a useful resource long after your holiday club has finished.

BIBLE TEACHING

The Professor, whether live or on video, will cover the following topics.

	THE ARTEFACT	FEATURED STORY	OVERVIEW	TYPE OF WRITING
Sunday 1	Sand	Joseph and his brothers settle in Egypt	Genesis – the creation – Adam and Eve – Noah – Abraham – Joseph and his brothers	The Beginning – the world – the nation of Israel
Day 1	A piece of stone with writing on it in Egypt	The Ten Commandments – the story of Moses	Exodus – Deuteronomy	Law
Day 2	A trumpet/ ram's horn	Joshua defeats Jericho	Joshua and Judges – Jericho – Gideon – Samson	History
Day 3	A nappy	Solomon judges between two women who both claim a baby	The first kings – Saul – David – Solomon Wisdom literature – Psalms and Proverbs	Poetry and Wisdom
Day 4	A clay pot	Jeremiah: The king cuts up Jeremiah's scroll	The divided kingdom – Israel and Judah – the prophets – the exile and return	Prophecy
Day 5	A grave cloth (and for non-video users, a Bible)	Jesus' death and resurrection	Jesus – his birth – miracles – teaching – his death and resurrection	Gospels
Sunday 2	A piece of parchment (part of a letter)	Paul's travels	The early church	Acts/Letters

THE MIGHTY GODSWORD!

On Day 5, the Desert Detectives finally find what they are looking for – the Mighty GodSword! But they don't realise it at the time because it's not what they are expecting. It's a book. In fact, it's a Bible, and they read the first part of Hebrews 4:12: 'For the word of God is living and active, sharper than any double-edged sword' (NIV). Then they realise that the valuable and powerful treasure isn't the Mighty GodSword, but the Mighty God's Word! The Bible is powerful and valuable because it's God's Word.

But that's not all! When the Professor reads John 1:14: 'The Word became a human being', he realises that the Mighty God's Word is Jesus, God's living Word. God didn't just *tell* people his Word; he *showed* them. And although God's living Word was killed, he rose again and is still living and active today! Jesus is not limited to being with one person in one place at one time, as in the desert. He is everywhere and can be with everyone.

EXPEDITION SHEETS AND THE DESERT DETECTIVES' NOTEBOOK

DESERT DETECTIVES has expedition (activity) sheets for each day – one for 5 to 7 year-olds, and one for the 8 to 11s. These have puzzles and questions that you can use in your small groups. These are essential for reinforcing the Bible story and helping children to read the Bible for themselves. Children colour and cut out the books from their expedition sheets and stick them on the empty bookshelves from page 49. The small group (tent group) time gives ample opportunity for tent leaders to relate to the children, talk about the Bible, talk with God and share the good news of Jesus.

The **DESERT DETECTIVES' NOTEBOOK** is an extra resource, available to help and encourage the children to explore the Bible on their own. It can be used in tent times or given to a child at the end of the holiday club. It's an A6, 48-page booklet, with a section on each of the different types of Bible writing to help children understand how the different sections and stories fit together.

Most of the pages in the notebook are activity pages. They contain:
– a Bible passage to look up
– a puzzle to explore the passage's content or meaning
– information

The **DESERT DETECTIVES' NOTEBOOK** is particularly suitable for children aged 8 to 11. Children who use Scripture Union's *Snapshots* Bible-reading notes will be familiar with the format. And for those who haven't come across *Snapshots*, the **DESERT DETECTIVES' NOTEBOOK** is an ideal way to introduce children to this type of material.

You can order the **DESERT DETECTIVES' NOTEBOOK**, or the quarterly *Snapshots* notes, direct from Scripture Union or from your local Christian bookshop. See the inside front cover and page 80 for details.

A SAMPLE TIMETABLE

The programme for the children is for two hours. It could be extended to two and a half hours with the addition of games and more time in the base camp and expeditions. The order of activities varies from day to day.

9:00– 9:30 30 minutes	9:30 – 9:40 10 minutes	9:40 – 10:20 40 minutes	10:20 – 11:00 40 minutes	11:00 – 11:20 20 minutes	11:20 – 11:30 10 minutes
	Small groups (tents)	All together (base camp)	Small groups (tents)	All together (base camp)	Small groups (tents)
Team preparation and prayer	Children arrive, register, and go straight to their tents to: Decorate their tents, or do their **DESERT DETECTIVES' NOTEBOOKS**.	Singing Drama Workout Desert Detectives Challenge Video/Professor	Back to the tent for: Oasis (refreshments) Craft Expeditions Discussion Prayer Filling in expedition sheets	Singing Memory verse Postbox Reviewing the morning	Back to tents to be collected

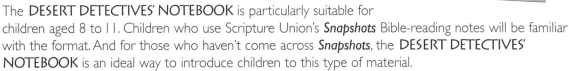

PART 2
Setting up a holiday club

THE PLANNING TEAM

All the helpers should be involved in planning and preparing for **Desert Detectives**. But you will need a smaller team to coordinate things and make some initial decisions. As well as the holiday club's overall leader, this should include your most experienced leaders, your minister and your children's workers. Most of the planning team will be part of the holiday club itself, but you may want to include others to make use of their particular gifts or experience.

AIMS

The broad aims of **Desert Detectives** are outlined on page 5, but you may have others. For example:

- attracting new children to join your children's Sunday groups or other children's activities
- developing your leaders' gifts and experience
- presenting the gospel to children who've never heard it
- providing an opportunity for children to make an initial or further commitment to follow Jesus
- getting to know the children in your church
- providing a project to encourage your church to work together
- establishing links with the children's families
- encouraging cooperation with other churches or groups in your area
- launching an ongoing mid-week children's group

Any or all of these aims may be appropriate, but you'll need to decide what you want **Desert Detectives** to achieve in your situation. And if you have several aims, you'll need to decide which are the most important. You'll need to evaluate **Desert Detectives** afterwards. How will you know whether you've met your aims?

THE CHILDREN

Having set your aims, you'll be able to make the other main decisions.

- Who you will invite to **Desert Detectives**.

- Do your aims primarily relate to the children already involved in your church, or those outside it?

- How many children do you want to involve? If your main aim is to get to know the children better, you might need to restrict numbers. On the other hand, if your main aim is to present the gospel to children who haven't heard it, you may want as many as possible to attend.

- Do you want to cater for an age-range that's well represented in your current groups, or one that isn't? Can you differentiate your activities for different ages, or do you need to have a fairly narrow age-range? Are your aims more suited to older children or younger ones? The core **Desert Detectives** age-range is 5 to 11, but suggestions are given for working with under-fives (page 77) and over-elevens (page 79).

DATES AND DURATION

You'll need to fix the date for your holiday club early enough for people to take it into account when they book their holidays and so that the dates do not clash with other holiday clubs in the area, activities already booked at your premises, holidays organised by local schools, holidays/camps for local Boys' Brigade, Girls' Brigade, Cub or Brownie groups, and carnivals or local events taking place in your area.

The potential leaders' availability will have most effect on the duration of your holiday club. If most of your leaders need to take time off work, it may not be practical to run a full five-day club.

Of course, there are many ways to use **Desert Detectives** – perhaps an after-school club, Saturday club or a Sunday teaching programme. Part 5 gives some ideas for adapting **Desert Detectives**.

LEADERS

There are many different roles for leaders in **Desert Detectives** (see page 13). Your leaders do not all have to be experienced children's workers. Many people in your church will be quite capable of leading a small group of children, after some initial basic training. And others will be suitable for supporting roles, such as musicians, registrars and providing refreshments. Of course, many of the leaders with these supporting roles may be group leaders as well. The table below shows the minimum recommended adult to child ratios.

ADULT TO CHILD RATIOS

The recommended adult to child ratios are as follows:

for 0–2 years – one adult to every 3 children (1:3)
for 2–3 years – one adult to every 4 children (1:4)
for 3–8 years – one adult to every 8 children (1:8)
for over-eights – one adult for the first 8 children, followed by one for every 12 (1:12).

There should always be more than one adult for any group and one should be female.

Desert Detectives is an ideal opportunity to develop and nurture the gifts and experience of the teenagers in your church, in a structured and supervised environment. Bear in mind, though, that for the purpose of child protection matters, a child is anyone under 18. In other words, if you have a number of teenage helpers, you will need *more* adult leaders, not less.

At first sight this seems odd, because teenage leaders can be extremely helpful and competent, and can therefore make the adult leader's job much easier. But it does make sense if we understand that even the most competent helpers will need to be mentored and encouraged if their gifts are to be developed to their full potential. We must avoid the temptation of only giving our younger helpers the mundane or less challenging tasks. And if we are aiming to stretch our helpers, then they will need the help and support of an adult leader.

APPOINTING AND TRAINING TEAM MEMBERS

As good practice, all team members should be made aware of the current legislation as it affects this kind of activity. The welfare of the children we hope to reach through **Desert Detectives** is of paramount importance. We are concerned for their spiritual welfare, but also of course for their physical and emotional welfare. Sadly nowadays, children are at risk as much as ever before, and it is our duty to do all we can to ensure their safety and well-being as we aim to show them God's love.

All churches should have clear child protection policies. If you have an established procedure for your church, all of the holiday club team must go through the process. If you haven't a procedure in place, a special club week may well be a good opportunity to establish one. The following notes outline the main issues.

UK LAW

(If using **Desert Detectives** elsewhere in the world, check current legislation and what is required.)

The government has published a code of practice for groups working with children. It is called **Safe from Harm**, and it contains a number of guidelines for good practice. Most denominations now have established good practice policies based on **Safe from Harm** and it is important that you work according to the one that applies to you. For further advice or information in the UK, contact the Churches' Child Protection Advisory Service on 01322 667207/660011.

Safe from Harm contains guidelines rather than law, but you need to show that you have taken them into consideration. In fact, if you ignore such good practice, your insurance may be invalid.

One important action is to ensure all those with access to children under eighteen (volunteers or in paid employment) make a signed declaration of any criminal conviction, including those 'spent' under the Rehabilitation of Offenders Act 1974, along with details of cautions, reprimands or warnings. Your denomination may decide to make use of the Criminal Records Bureau, which is due to start functioning in England and Wales at the end of 2001. CCPAS can advise you on this too.

Failure to take the necessary steps could lead to a claim of negligence against the church if a child comes to any harm at the hand of anyone working with them in a voluntary capacity. 'Harm' includes ill-treatment of any kind (including sexual abuse), or impairment of physical or mental health or development.

You should ask all potential team members to sign a form such as the one below. Emphasise that it represents positive action for good practice, and does not imply any slur or suspicion. Obviously the nature of the form is sensitive and should be handled with care. Ensure that confidentiality is maintained. In accordance with the Data Protection Act, do not divulge any information to third parties.

If anyone gives a 'yes' answer, allow the individual to explain this disclosure personally or by letter. If you are in any doubt about the person's suitability, consult your church leader.

As well as the declaration form, it is recommended that potential team members offer one name as a referee. Questions to ask a referee might include:

— in what capacity have you known the applicant, and for how long?
— how willing and able is he/she to work with others?
— how suitable would you consider him/her for work with children and young people?
— are there any relevant details about this applicant which cause you concern?

Do not allow people not known to you to have unsupervised access to the children.

CONFIDENTIAL DECLARATION FOR POTENTIAL TEAM MEMBERS

Guidelines from the Home Office following the Children Act 1989 advise that all voluntary organisations, including churches, take steps to safeguard the children who are entrusted to their care. You are therefore asked to make the following declarations:

Do you have any current or spent criminal convictions, cautions, bindovers or cases pending? **Yes** ☐ **No** ☐

Have you ever been held liable by a court for a civil wrong, or had an order made against you by a matrimonial or a family court? **Yes** ☐ **No** ☐

Has your conduct ever caused, or been likely to cause, harm to a child or put a child at risk, or, to your knowledge, has it ever been alleged that your conduct has resulted in any of these things? **Yes** ☐ **No** ☐

Signed _____ Date _____

Because of the nature of the work for which you are applying, this post is exempt from the provision of Section 4(i) of the Rehabilitation of Offenders Act 1974, by virtue of the Rehabilitation of Offenders Act 1974 (Exemptions) Order 1975, and you are therefore not entitled to withhold information about convictions which, for other purposes, are 'spent' under the provisions of the Act. In the event of an appointment, any failure to disclose such convictions could result in the withdrawal of approval to work with children in the church.

OTHER ASPECTS OF TRAINING

You should allow for at least two training sessions, which are more or less compulsory.

In **Session one** you will want to explore your objectives for **Desert Detectives** and how it fits into a broader strategy. You will also want to look at working safely with children, building relationships with them, using the Bible with children (see page 58) and praying with them (see page 73). Spend time thinking about a child's world and what they will make of the stories and themes of the week. If you are likely to have children from other faith backgrounds, spend time preparing yourselves appropriately (see page 63).

In **Session two** you will need to look at the practicalities of working as a team, setting up the programme, which museum artefacts or frieze you are going to make, become familiar with the song and the video, and so on. Leave plenty of time for questions and prayer.

VENUE

You'll need a venue with enough space for the number of children and the activities you have in mind. If your own premises are not large enough, you may be able to use a local school or other hall. If you do, try to book it for a few days prior to the actual holiday club week, so that you have time to set up the stage, scenery etc.

UK LAW

Even if you don't need to register your holiday club under the Children Act, carefully consider the following requirements laid down by the Act as sensible guidelines to be interpreted with common sense. If you must register you won't have any choice!

Requirements for accommodation state that the premises should be warm, clean and adequately lit and ventilated, with clearly marked emergency exits. The minimum unencumbered floor space to be provided for children aged 5 to 8 years is 25 square feet (2.3 square metres) per child. In other words, be careful about very large numbers of children in a small hall and work out the maximum number of children who can attend.

The premises you use should meet Health and Safety requirements. Check that the owners of the premises have complied with all the requirements. Ideally there should be one toilet and one hand basin for every ten children. Disposable towels or hot-air hand driers are preferable to roller towels. If you are preparing food on site, you will need to be inspected by the Environmental Health Officer. The person with overall responsibility for the catering arrangements should have the minimum of the Basic Food and Hygiene Certificate. Smoking should not be permitted on the premises. Children should not be allowed unsupervised access to the kitchen.

LAYING OUT YOUR ROOM(S)

Some activities take place in one large group and others in a number of small groups. Whether you have one room or lots, you'll need to allocate space for both these types of activities.

Most of the action is led from the front, so you'll need a 'stage' area, and a large area for the children to sit. The 'stage' area must be big enough for your drama scenery and props such as a tent or sandpit, as well as your music stands and any large musical instruments such as drums or keyboards. If you are not using the video, you'll also need an area for the Professor's Bible bookcase.

The seating area will need to be quite big. Each child will need enough room to sit comfortably, as well as to join in with action songs and aerobic exercises when they are standing up. This space can be used much more flexibly if the children sit on the floor rather than on chairs. It is important that team members sit with children, not only for the purposes of discipline but also for adults and children alike to share the experience of **Desert Detectives**. It is important for relationship-building.

Each small group will need its own area, with enough space to do the craft and activity sheets, and to talk comfortably as a group. Entrance to the tent and the walls can be made as tent-like as possible but avoid any structure that might be hazardous. This will be the children's 'den' for the week.

Here is an example of how a single hall might be set out for the various activities. There are more suggestions on page 15.

SUGGESTED ROOM LAYOUT

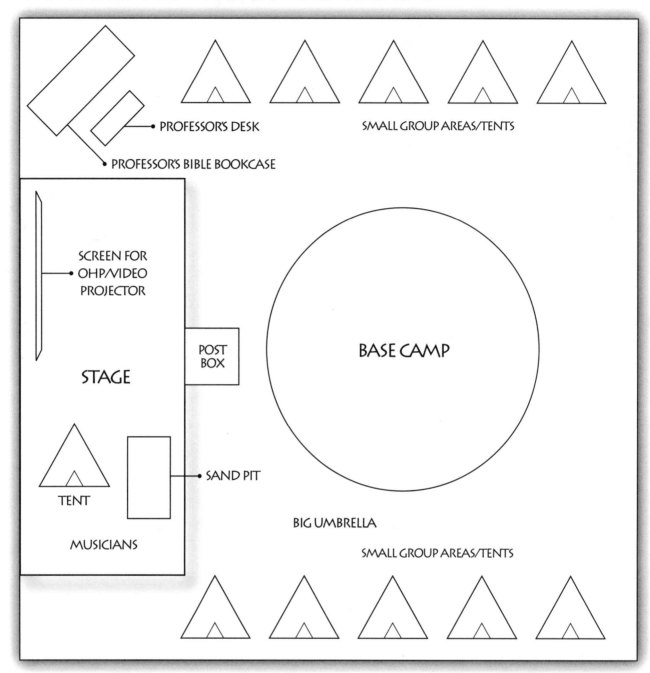

PROFESSOR'S DESK

PROFESSOR'S BIBLE BOOKCASE

SMALL GROUP AREAS/TENTS

SCREEN FOR OHP/VIDEO PROJECTOR

STAGE

POST BOX

BASE CAMP

TENT

SAND PIT

MUSICIANS

BIG UMBRELLA

SMALL GROUP AREAS/TENTS

FINANCES

You'll need to consider your financial resources. Work out what you'll need money for. Examples might include:

— craft materials
— refreshments
— materials for the scenery
— photocopying/printing costs
— hire of premises
— hire of equipment such as video projector
— **DESERT DETECTIVES** books for your leaders
— resources such as the **DESERT DETECTIVES VIDEO** and **DESERT DETECTIVES' NOTEBOOKS.**

Do you now need to do some fund-raising? Or will you charge a small fee for children attending **Desert Detectives**?

Who does what – key tasks

REGISTRATION

To make sure **Desert Detectives** isn't over-subscribed, you'll need children to register beforehand. Appoint someone with specific responsibility to coordinate the registration process. Devise a registration form, and a parent's/guardian's/carer's consent form. You may also need an invitation card or introductory letter.

SAMPLE REGISTRATION FORM

DESERT DETECTIVES REGISTRATION FORM (please use a separate form for each child)	
Desert Detectives will take place at *(venue)* from *(start date)* to *(end date)* (give times) Please fill in this form to book a place for your child.	
Child's full name	Sex: M/F
Date of birth · School	
Please register my child for Desert Detectives. Parent's/Guardian's signature	
Parent's/Guardian's full name	
Address	
Phone number	
Nearer to the event, parents/guardians will need to fill in a consent form. *I give permission for my details to be entered on the church database.	

SAMPLE CONSENT FORM

DESERT DETECTIVES CONSENT FORM (please use a separate form for each child)	
Child's full name	Date of birth
Address	
Emergency contact name	Phone number
GP's name	GP's Phone number
Any known allergies or conditions	

I confirm that the above details are complete and correct to the best of my knowledge.

In the unlikely event of illness or accident I give permission for any necessary medical treatment to be given by the nominated first-aider. In an emergency and if I cannot be contacted, I am willing for my child to receive hospital treatment, including anaesthetic if necessary. I understand that every effort will be made to contact me as soon as possible.

Parent's/Guardian's signature · Date

PRINTING AND PUBLICITY

Although the registration coordinator will be responsible for issuing and collating the above forms, they may not be the best person to design and produce them. It is good to have a small team responsible for all of the printed material related to **Desert Detectives**. It's tempting to think that this isn't needed, as many people have computers at home, which easily produce letters and posters. But this is precisely the problem – computers make it very easy to produce poor materials. They may have good typefaces and a wide variety of quality clip art, but these elements do not guarantee a good publication; just as a good cooker and quality ingredients do not guarantee a culinary masterpiece!

A dedicated design team will ensure that any material connected with **Desert Detectives** has a uniform look and feel, with all forms and letters having the same few typefaces and similar layout. Clip art can be coordinated so that the style of the various pictures is compatible, and logos can be used consistently in terms of size, position and colour. The **Desert Detectives** logo below can be photocopied. It is also on the **Desert Detectives** website and you can download it. See page 2 for details.

Promotional and other material is available from CPO. See inside back cover for details.

A design team could be responsible for:

— **posters and flyers**: to advertise **Desert Detectives**

— **helpers' forms**: for potential team members to indicate the roles they'd like to do. This could include the declaration outlined on page 10

— **helper's notes or training materials**: even if someone else writes this material, the design team should be responsible for the layout

— **name badges**: even if the children design and make their own badges, team members need a pre-designed badge, so that they can be readily identified

— **signs and notices**: your building may need signs to indicate relevant entrances, toilets and any areas that are out of bounds. These should use the same typeface and colours as other materials to maintain the **Desert Detectives** theme, even when the children are not in the main room

— **prayer cards/bookmarks**: prayer pointers to help church members to pray for the holiday club before, during and after **Desert Detectives** events.

PROPS AND SCENERY

Children don't just want to hear about an adventure: they want to have one! When they come to **Desert Detectives**, they are entering an imaginary desert as they become involved in the search for the Mighty GodSword. Children are usually good at using their imaginations, but you can help them by using yours!

TAKE THE STAGE

Your stage area will be the focus of attention for much of **Desert Detectives**, for this is where the drama takes place. You'll need a backdrop to disguise your wall. Paint some yellow dunes on the bottom half and blue sky at the top.

 Collect old sheets and sew them together to make a large backcloth, or make lightweight, portable stage flats by stretching canvas over timber frames. Make these approximately 240 cm by 120 cm, (8' x 4') and hinge them in pairs so that they can be free-standing.

For the drama, you'll also need:

- a ridge tent or frame tent, depending on the space available. Preferably old, faded, and khaki in colour. The **Desert Detectives** logo could be attached to this.
- some sand… and something to put it in.

 Use proper play sand. Don't be tempted to use building sand, as it can stain your presenters' clothes. The sandpit should be long enough for two people side-by-side to dig in, but it doesn't have to be very wide. (They can stand behind it, rather than in it.) Fill one or more strong, shallow cardboard boxes. On the front, stick a long piece of card or hardboard, cut to look like a small dune, and painted yellow to match the backdrop.

 Use similar 'dunes' to hide large stage furniture, such as keyboard, drum kit and video or overhead projector. Using the same method, make cactuses, snakes etc to hide smaller items like music stands.

CANVAS OPINIONS

The other main place where children spend time is in their small group area. Make each group area look like a tent, using old sheets. Children can draw on their tents or pin things on to them to make them all different. Each group could choose a name and make its own flag. Alternatively have a large ground sheet for each group which they put down for their tent time each day.

OUT OF THIS WORLD

Try to avoid children having to leave the desert world when they use corridors between rooms, or when they go to the toilet. Decorate these rooms with camels and palm trees too, or at least use signs in an appropriate style for the theme.

DRESS IT UP

Leaders should dress appropriately. Not just the presenters but *all* the leaders. For example, khaki shorts and shirts, sunglasses and sun hats, water bottles.

NAME NAMES

Use appropriate words and names, for example 'oasis' instead of refreshment area, 'tent' instead of small group, 'base camp' for the main meeting area.

DETAILS

Pay attention to the details and enter into the fun of a desert expedition. For example, use a sand-timer for games instead of a watch. Leaders could drink from water bottles rather than cups for their oasis.

PROFESSOR'S BOOKCASE

Allow plenty of time to collect 66 old telephone books and catalogues to make the Bible books. Make covers from coloured paper (see page 33).

CRAFT

Although the craft takes place in the small tent groups, a dedicated craft preparation team can be very useful, especially in the run-up to **Desert Detectives**. This team can collect together necessary materials, as well as essential items such as pencils and glue sticks. They can make templates and patterns for children to draw round or cut out. The craft team should make up a sample of each craft for the children's tent leaders.

Different tent leaders may want to make different things. Encourage individual initiative and creativity. A few basic craft ideas are given for each day's programme. To reinforce the idea that the Bible is one big story rather than lots of unrelated stories, it would be a good idea for each child to do one craft activity which builds throughout the week, rather than a different one each day. Here are some suggestions.

BIBLE TIMELINE

Add pictures, poems and collages to a long strip of wallpaper to make a Bible timeline. This would be a good combined project for all of the under-sevens.

BIBLE BOOKSHELF

Make a bookshelf using stiff card and decorate it. Make 66 Bible books by covering matchboxes with paper or card (colour-coded for each type of writing). Write the name of each book on its spine. A different section could be added each day to reflect that day's theme. This is particularly suited to over-eights, but it is only practical for a relatively small number of children due to the large number of matchboxes required!

BIBLE MUSEUM

Children make or bring in 'artefacts' to represent Bible stories. They could cover boxes with cling film to make display cases, and write labels for the museum visitor. The museum could then be opened for parents and visitors during the following weekend. This is particularly suitable for the oldest children. You will need to choose the best artefacts.

SECURITY

It is important to have a registration team to welcome children so that tent leaders are free to talk with their groups, and presenters and musicians can concentrate on the session to come.

If you have a large holiday club, or if you are inviting a number of children who have no other contact with your church, it can be difficult to know whether the person collecting a child is the person who is authorised to do so. In such a situation a form of 'receipt' slip is useful.

On the next page is an example of the front and reverse of such a slip. The instructions on the reverse explain how it works.

If, when dropping off the child, the parent signs the reverse to say that their child may go home alone or with someone else, the registrar should give that slip to the child's tent leader during the session.

If a person wants to collect a child but neither they nor the group leader has the slip, they should be referred to the club's leader who will make sure that they are authorised to collect the child before allowing them to do so.

OTHER SUPPORT ROLES

FIRST AID

A first aid kit must be easily accessible and at least one member of your team should have a working knowledge of first aid.

You must record any accidents or incidents in an accident book. This is essential in the event of any insurance claim. A record of the matter should be noted, along with details of action taken. It should be countersigned where appropriate.

Everyone should be made aware of emergency procedures and fire exits, and there must be access to a telephone. This could be a mobile phone, if necessary.

REFRESHMENTS

This team will be responsible for obtaining and preparing the refreshments and for tidying up afterwards. If your holiday club is large and your budget allows, use disposable cups to avoid excessive washing up. Check that you have no children with food allergies. Drinks can be served in their tents from large plastic bottles.

SAMPLE COLLECTION SLIP

FRONT

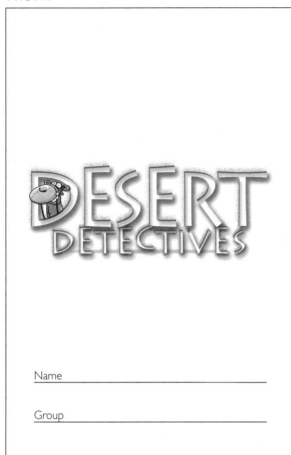

Name _____

Group _____

BACK

Please make sure that you collect this slip when you bring your child each day. You will need it to collect your child at the end of the morning. If your child is to be collected by someone else, please pass on this slip to that person.

If you will be unable to do this, or if your child is to go home on his/her own, please note this below, and return the slip to the registration desk immediately.

☐ Tick here if your child may go home on his/her own

☐ Tick here if someone else is to collect your child. Write his/her name next to the day concerned.

Monday _____

Tuesday _____

Wednesday _____

Thursday _____

Friday _____

Thank you for your cooperation.

In the event of an emergency, the church telephone number is *(insert your number)*

TECHNICAL

If you are using a full public address system, with various musicians and presenters, you'll probably need someone to mix the sound and keep an eye on the microphones. Even in a small club, it's helpful to have someone specifically responsible for items such as TVs, videos or overhead projectors.

If you have less than 50 children, one or two TV sets can be used to show the video. To link two sets, you'll need a coaxial cable and a 'splitter', so that the video signal can be sent to both TVs. If you have more than 50 children you should consider using a video projector. Either way, the sound will be better if played through your PA system rather than from the TVs or projector.

GROUP LEADERS

The tent leader's role is to get to know the children so that they feel welcome and comfortable at **Desert Detectives**, to enable the children to explore God's Word together in a way that relates specifically to them. There are a number of activities for the tent times, but these should be flexible. It is far more important to have meaningful discussions with the children in your group than it is to complete all the activities.

Young or inexperienced team members can be assistant leaders. This helps the group leader, as well as allowing the assistants to develop their own gifts and skills under supervision.

If you have a large holiday club, you may need to organise the tent groups into expeditions of six to eight groups. An expedition leader would not ideally have a tent group of their own, so that they are free to oversee all of the groups and leaders in their expedition.

Let your team members know that it is not appropriate for them to talk to children alone in a secluded place – it might be misinterpreted. Sadly, touching children is not advisable now, although the government has made it clear that such actions as guiding with a hand on the shoulder or comforting a distressed young child would not be considered inappropriate. It is a question of common sense in this area, but if in doubt, don't! You must have an agreed procedure in the case of a child disclosing abuse or a situation which puts them at risk.

The tent leaders have a specific responsibility for the children in their tent during the week. They will sit with them on all occasions, answering their questions and prompting them to discover more about the big story of God's Word and Jesus, the Word made human!

PRESENTERS

Ideally, your presenters will be the three actors in the drama – Sandy, Doug and June, so they will be in role throughout the base camp sessions. They may also introduce aerobics or other parts of the programme. Or you may use other people for this.

MUSICIANS

It's good to have a number of musicians playing a variety of instruments, but you'll need to make sure you have enough stage space for other things too! A holiday club is an ideal opportunity to introduce new songs, but don't try to introduce too many. Include some old favourites as well.

The DESERT DETECTIVES SONG

Down in the desert, a long way away,
There's treasure buried there, we've heard people say
So we're travelling abroad
And we're looking for the Mighty GodSword

We're looking over here, we're looking over there
Down low, up high, we're looking everywhere
And we won't stop trying
'Til we've found the Mighty GodSword

'Cause the Mighty GodSword is powerful
And its wisdom makes you wise
And there never was a treasure that ever was better.
It's the very best ever prize!

The Mighty GodSword

Steve Burnhope
arr. Gill Hutchinson

Use first 8 bars as intro and between. Repeat chorus to end.

DRAMA SCRIPTS – DOUG, SANDY AND JUNE

MEET THE DESERT DETECTIVES

June: the leader, but very lazy. Tends to delegate all the work to the other two.

Doug: a bit of a know-it-all, but in fact he's not very bright. He also tends to do disgusting things.

Sandy: easily bored and easily scared. Doesn't really want to be there.

PROPS

- Three shovels or spades. Large beach spades are ideal. For safety, use plastic spades rather than metal ones
- An envelope or parcel, big enough to hold each day's 'find'. A large brown Jiffy bag is ideal

DRAMA (EPISODE A)

Either for use on the first Sunday service or as Part 1 of the drama on Day 1 to introduce the Professor, the Mighty GodSword and the characters.

PROPS YOU NEED FOR THIS EPISODE

- A sheet of sandpaper with a cross ('X') marked in the centre
- A large cross-shape ('X') cut from card – the same colour and shape as the one on the sandpaper
- A large spot shape, the same size as the cross

SCRIPT

(Enter the Desert Detectives)

June: Come on Doug! Come on Sandy! Keep up!

Sandy: But June, I'm sure we're going the wrong way!

June: Well, we've been following the map. Look! *(Holds up a piece of sandpaper)*

Doug: No wonder we're lost: you've got the map upside down!
(He turns the map the right way up, which of course makes no difference at all)

Sandy: I knew we were going the wrong way. We'll never find the position marked by that 'eX'.

June: Oh yes we will. Look, here it is! *(She picks up a large cross from the ground)*

Doug: eX-cellent! We've arrived! That's what the Professor said: 'eX marks the spot.'

June: *(Picking up a large spot)* He was right. Look: here's the spot!

Sandy: Great! We've found the spot we were looking for! Can we go home now?

June: No, we can't go until we find the Mighty GodSword.

Sandy: The Mighty GodSword? What's that?

June: It's what the Professor sent us to look for. It's an ancient and powerful treasure.

Sandy: So why does the Professor think the Mighty GodSword is here?

Doug: *(Holding up the cross and the spot)* Because it's eX-tremely valuable, and the Professor thinks that if we dig here, we might spot it.

June: Right then. You two start digging, while I eat jam-in-my-sandwiches, and dessert.

Sandy: While you what?!

June: Oh, er ... I said, "While I examine the sand-which-is ... in the desert." *(June exits)*

Doug: Right then, let's start digging.

(Doug and Sandy begin to dig, side-by-side. But without realising it, each one shovels their waste sand into the other person's hole. They continue like this for some time. Hopefully the children will notice and tell them what they're doing. If they do, Doug and Sandy should interact with the children to realise their mistake, and miss out the indented part below)

Sandy: *(Stops digging and watches Doug for a while)*
Hey! Stop digging for a minute.

Doug: Why? What's up?

Sandy: Look! You're shovelling all your sand into my hole.

Doug: What hole? There is no hole!

Sandy: Exactly! Just stand still for a moment and let me dig.
(Sandy digs as before, emptying his sand into Doug's hole)

Sandy: There! That's a whole lot better!

Doug: No, it isn't! Look: you've been filling in my hole too!

(Only include the following if this is part of the Sunday service)

Sandy: Look out! Here comes June. *(Sandy hands the envelope to Doug)* Quick, make a sand parcel.

(Sandy takes out a piece of paper and begins to write. Meanwhile, Doug takes out a bucket and spade and starts to make a sandcastle)

Doug: There isn't any water for the moat!

Sandy: I'm writing the note: you just worry about the parcel.

Doug: I didn't say, 'note': I said, 'moat' – for my sandcastle.

Sandy: Sandcastle? I didn't say, 'sandcastle': I said, 'sand parcel'. Fill that parcel with sand. And hurry up!

(Doug fills the parcel. June returns, stretching and rubbing her eyes as if she's just woken up)

Doug: Hello June, why are you rubbing your eyes?

June: I've been sleeping. I mean, er… sweeping. Yes: sweeping… I've, er… got sand in my eyes. *(She quickly changes the subject)* Anyway, have you dug up anything interesting?

(Doug and Sandy reply 'No' and 'Yes' respectively, both at the same time. Sandy surreptitiously hits Doug with his shovel)

Sandy: Yes: we've put it in the parcel, with a note to send to the Professor.

Doug: But Sandy, the parcel's full of sand. *(Sandy hits him with the shovel again)*

Sandy: Yes, we've, er… padded it with sand to keep it safe.

June: Excellent! Come on then! Let's go and send it.

(June and Sandy exit. Doug follows behind, peering into the parcel and looking puzzled)

DRAMA (EPISODE 1)

If most of the children haven't seen Episode A, include it here, but miss out the last part about the sand parcel. At the point where Sandy says, 'Look out! Here comes June', go straight into Episode 1. Or you could perform each episode separately, with another activity in between. Episode 1 is important because it sets the scene by introducing the characters and their quest for the Mighty GodSword.

PROPS YOU NEED FOR THIS EPISODE

– A roll of white toilet paper
– A piece of a stone slab (such as a paving stone)

SCRIPT

(Enter the Desert Detectives, if they are not already on stage. June is clutching her stomach as if in pain)

June: Ooh! Ouch! I knew I was mad to have another cake.

Sandy: What was that?

June: Er… I said, 'I've got a bad stomach ache.' I think I'd better go to the toilet.

Doug: OK. We'll wait for you.

June: Oh, don't worry about me. I think you should start digging without me. I'm sure I won't be too long!

(June exits. Doug and Sandy start digging)

Doug: I wonder what we'll find today. Hopefully the Mighty GodSword!

Sandy: I hope we don't find anything nasty. It's scary when June isn't here to look after us.

Doug: *(Throughout this speech, Doug is thinking aloud. He is completely unaware that Sandy is becoming more and more frightened)*

Don't be silly Sandy: there's nothing to be scared of here.

Except the vultures of course…   *(Sandy scans the sky anxiously)*

But they're not really interested in you
unless you're dead.   *(Sandy breathes a sigh of relief)*

Which you might be, of course,
if the scorpions get you!   *(Sandy looks scared again)*

But you should be OK…   *(Sandy breathes another sigh of relief)*

You just have to make sure they don't
crawl into your boots in the night.   *(Sandy quickly takes his boots off)*

The tarantulas are worse. Sometimes they
crawl up your shovel and up your sleeve.   *(Sandy drops his shovel and shakes his clothes)*

But you needn't worry about the tarantulas… *(Sandy looks relieved)*

The snakes will probably get them.   *(Sandy leaps into Doug's arms)*

Sandy: I want my mummy!

Doug: *(Putting Sandy down)* You might be in luck, Sandy. It looks like there's a mummy here.

Sandy: What! My mummy?!

Doug: No: an Egyptian mummy!

Sandy: *(Leaping into Doug's arms again)* W… w… where?!

Doug: *(Putting Sandy down again)* Look, here in the sand. Here's its bandage.
(He pulls out a length of white toilet paper)

(June returns, walking in a funny way)

June: Oh, that's where the toilet paper is! I couldn't find it, so I had to wipe my bottom on a passing scorpion. It doesn't half sting!

Doug: That must have been a shock! You'd better sit down for a while to get over it.

June: Yes. I could do with a rest! *(She sits down, but leaps up in pain and clutches her bottom)* Ouch! Perhaps I'll just stand here instead.

Sandy: You could always do some digging! Then we'd get to the bottom quicker.

June: Bottom? *(She rubs hers)* Ooh! Don't talk to me about bottoms!

(Sandy and Doug continue to dig)

Sandy: Hey! What's this?

Doug: What? Is it the Mighty GodSword?

Sandy: Oh, false alarm. It's just a piece of stone. *(He throws it away, but June retrieves it)*

June: Wait a minute! It's got some words on it.

Doug: What does it say?

June: It's very faded, but it looks like, 'Donut-covered donkey'.

Sandy: That doesn't make sense!

Doug: It makes sense to me!

June: What, 'Donut-covered donkey'?

Doug: Yes. I reckon that the ancient people would have put donuts on their donkeys. Then, if the mule train got stuck in traffic they could have a jammy snack. That's probably where the phrase 'traffic jam' comes from!

June: What complete rubbish! I think we'd better send this to the Professor for a more sensible explanation. Come on! *(They stick the stone into a padded envelope, and exit)*

DRAMA (EPISODE 2)

PROPS YOU NEED FOR THIS EPISODE

- A personal stereo with large headphones
- A metal detector (if you haven't got a real one, this can be improvised using a vacuum cleaner extension, or broomstick with a box attached half-way up and a disk of card at the bottom)
- Sound effects for the metal detector. One way to make a 'beeping' sound is by repeatedly pressing a high pitched note on a keyboard. Or make a 'buzzer' sound using a kazoo or electric guitar
- Doug should wear boots
- A trumpet or a ram's horn (if you want to be really authentic). If you don't have a trumpet or bugle, use a cone made from gold or silver card)

SCRIPT

(Enter June, dancing and wearing headphones, apparently using a metal detector)

(Enter Doug and Sandy)

Sandy: Have you found anything yet with your metal detector, June?
(June doesn't hear and continues as before) June! *(Still no response)* JUNE! *(June stops and removes the headphones)*

Doug: What are you doing, June?

June: I'm listening to heavy metal. I mean... I'm looking for heavy metal.

Doug: Can I have a go? *(Before June can protest, he puts on the headphones and takes*

23

the metal detector) Oh! I can hear drums and guitars! I think there must be some musical instruments buried here!

Sandy: Let me have a listen. *(He takes the metal detector and headphones from Doug)* You're right, there is music. Hold on a minute… this metal detector isn't switched on. And these headphones are attached to June's personal stereo!

June: I was just having a little rest.

Sandy: *(Plugging the headphones into the detector)* Let's try using this properly. *(He searches for a while, but nothing happens)* No, there's nothing here.

Doug: Let me have a go. *(Doug checks exactly the same area as Sandy, but this time the detector beeps furiously)*

Sandy: I think he's found something!

June: *(Handing Sandy a shovel)* Yes, you'd better dig and see what's there. Perhaps it's the Mighty GodSword.

Sandy: *(After digging for a while)* No. There's nothing here.

Doug: *(Doug checks a different area, and again the detector beeps furiously)* Try over here, Sandy.

Sandy: *(After digging)* No. There's nothing here, either.

(Doug tries another place, and the detector beeps again)

June: Dig over there, Sandy.

Sandy: *(Getting suspicious)* Hold on. Let me have another go with the metal detector. *(Sandy sweeps the same area again but this time the metal detector doesn't make a sound. Doug walks across to Sandy and the detector beeps. He walks away and it stops. This happens a few times)*

Sandy: Doug's making it beep! He must be made of metal. Help! Doug's a robot! *(He runs and hides behind June)*

June: Don't be silly, Sandy. Robots are intelligent. Doug couldn't possibly be a robot!

Doug: That's right!

June: Look, I'll prove it. *(She points the detector at Doug's head)* See, he hasn't got a metal brain.

Sandy: But his brain's probably too small to be detected. You'd better check the rest of him.

(June checks Doug from head to toe. It only beeps when the detector goes near his feet)

June: What have you got in your boots, Doug?

Doug: Erm… my feet!

Sandy: Your boots have got steel toecaps, haven't they?

Doug: *(Suddenly realising)* Oh yeah; they have.

June: You mean your boots were making the metal detector beep?

Sandy: We'll never find the Mighty GodSword if Doug's boots keep setting off the metal detector!

June: Sandy's right, Doug. You'll have to take them off. *(Doug sits down and takes his boots off)*

Sandy: Phew! Your feet stink!

Doug: Can't help it: I forgot to pack a spare pair of socks!

June: But we left three months ago! Do you mean to say you haven't changed your socks for three months?

Doug: Of course I have. My socks fell apart six weeks ago, so I borrowed a pair of yours. Here, you can have them back now. *(He holds them out, near to June's face. June and Sandy both run away, holding their noses.)*

Sandy: Go and stand over there, so you're downwind of us!

(Doug gets up, but when his bare feet touch the hot sand, he dances about in pain, constantly hopping from one foot to the other)

Doug: Ooh! Ouch! This sand is really hot! Ooh! Ouch! Ooh! Ouch! I'd better go back to the tent. Ooh! Ouch! Ooh! Ouch! *(Doug exits, still hopping)* Ooh! Ouch! Ooh! Ouch! Ooh! Ouch…

June: It's no good, we'll have to bury those socks before they poison us.

Sandy: Good idea, I'll dig a hole.

June: Make sure it's a deep one! We wouldn't want them to escape! *(Sandy digs)*

Sandy: Hang on! I've found something: look! *(He digs up a ram's horn or an old and battered trumpet, full of sand)*
Let's see if it works. *(Sandy blows it. It makes no sound but blows sand all over June)*

June: *(Confiscates the trumpet)* I think I'll look after that. Come on, let's go and send it to the Professor for analysis.

(June and Sandy pack the ram's horn trumpet into a package, and exit)

DRAMA (EPISODE 3)

This episode involves a lot of slapstick. It must be rehearsed thoroughly as good timing is vital: both for the benefit of the audience and the safety of the actors!

PROPS YOU NEED FOR THIS EPISODE
- A personal stereo with large headphones from Episode 2
- A rake
- A snake (use a soft toy, a draught excluder or a large rubber snake. Or make one by stuffing a fabric cylinder and attaching eyes)
- A nappy, liberally filled with brown sauce or chocolate sauce so that it looks 'used'
- A knife (made of plastic or card: not a real one!)

SCRIPT

(Doug and Sandy are digging. June is listening to music on the headphones again and raking half-heartedly)

Sandy: I'm bored with digging. I don't think we're ever going to find the Mighty GodSword.

Doug: Hang on! I think I've found something! Pass the rake please, June. *(No response from June)*

Sandy: JUNE! *(June looks up, but doesn't remove the headphones)*

Doug: Pass the rake, please.

June: Pass the what?

Doug: The RAKE!

June: Are you sure?

Doug: Yes, hurry up! *(He holds out his arm to receive the rake, but he doesn't look at June because he's peering into the hole)*

June: OK, if you're sure. *(She passes a snake, which Doug takes without looking)* I don't know why you want a snake though!

Doug: Snake? I said rake.

(Doug looks at the snake, screams, and throws it away. But he throws it towards Sandy, who panics and tries to give it back to Doug. One ends up holding the snake's tail, and the other its head. They yell some more, and try to run away in opposite directions, but neither lets go of the snake. The effect is like holding elastic: after they have run as far as they can, the snake brings them back together and they collide. Doug lets go and the snake gets wrapped around Sandy's neck. Sandy acts as if it is choking him. During this, June notices what's happening and takes off her headphones)

Doug: Don't worry Sandy, I'll hit it with my shovel.

June: Noooo!

(Doug takes a swipe at Sandy's head with his shovel. Sandy ducks just in time. This is repeated a few times)

Doug: Wonder if it's poisonous?

Sandy: Poisonous?!!

June: It's all right, it isn't poisonous.

Doug: Good! That means we can eat it! I'll make a snake and kidney pie. Now, where's my big knife?
(He produces a large knife and advances towards Sandy)

June: Stop, you'll hurt him!

Sandy: Yes, you'll hurt me!

June: Didn't mean you. I meant Crusher!

Doug: Crusher!?

June: Yes, Crusher: my pet snake! *(She removes the snake from Sandy's neck, and gives it a cuddle)* Poor Crusher! Did the nasty man hurt you? It's all right, Mummy's here my darling!

Sandy: Your 'darling' just nearly killed me!

June: Don't be silly. He was just being friendly, weren't you, Crusher?

Sandy: *(Rubbing his neck)* Well, I think your pet snake is a pain in the neck!

June: Why did you want a snake anyway, Doug?

Doug: I didn't. I wanted a rake.

June: Well, why didn't you say so? It's over there. *(Doug retrieves the rake, and uses it)*

Doug: Look, there's something here. *(Sandy and June bend down to look at the ground near Doug's feet)*

Sandy: Phew! There's a horrible smell down here.

June: Have you taken your socks off again, Doug?

Doug: No, I've got my boots on this time. Hold on, I'll rake it some more. *(He does. Sandy and June hold their noses and move away to a safe distance)*

Doug: Look! It's a nappy! And it's got brown stuff in it! *(He holds it up to show them, letting the sauce run down a bit)* I wonder if that's what I think it is? *(He dips his finger into the sauce and licks it.)* Hmm, I'm not sure. *(He scratches his chin thoughtfully, thus getting sauce all over his chin)*

June: We'll have to send it to the Professor. Sandy, get the parcel. *(Sandy gets the parcel, and gingerly advances towards Doug, holding the parcel at arm's length in front of him, and holding his nose with the other hand. Doug drops the nappy into the parcel.)*

June: Come on, if we're quick we'll just catch the last post-camel. *(They exit)*

DRAMA (EPISODE 4)

In this episode, the Desert Detectives break a water pipe, and water spurts up from their hole. There are various ways to achieve this. If you have made a 'sand dune' (see page 15) an extra person could lie behind it with a water gun. If you are using a church that has a baptistry under the stage, someone could be out of sight in the baptistery (but make sure no one falls down it!). If neither is possible, you could bury a squeezy bottle in the sand, and one of the characters could subtly squeeze it at the right moment. You could maybe even use a small hose, if you only turn it on very slightly! Whatever method you use, make sure the water is kept away from any electrical equipment such as your video player or overhead projector!

PROPS YOU NEED FOR THIS EPISODE

- A tin mug
- A water bottle
- The metal detector from Episode 2
- A rake
- Something that will squirt water (see above)
- A clay pot

SCRIPT

(Doug and Sandy are digging as usual)

Doug: Where's June got to? We've been digging for three hours now and there's been no sign of her!

June: *(Entering)* Good morning, boys!

Sandy: Good afternoon, you mean.

June: I've got a good feeling about today. I reckon today might be the day we find the Mighty GodSword. Come on! Let's get digging!

Sandy: You mean you're actually going to do some digging?

June: Of course! Don't I always? Oh yes, there's nothing like a good dig to keep you fit and healthy! *(She digs vigorously. The other two join in)*

June: *(After about half a minute)* Phew! This digging is hard work! I need a rest!

Doug: It's thirsty work too. Pour me some water please, Sandy. *(Sandy pours the water bottle into a mug, but only sand comes out)*

Sandy: Uh-oh! It looks like we've run out of water.

June: Well, I knew it was getting low. We haven't had any water to wash in for ages.

Doug: Haven't we? I hadn't noticed!

Sandy: That's because you never wash!

Doug: But I need a drink!

June: Me too, I'm dripping with sweat!

Doug: Dripping? Hey! June's got some water. *(He licks some of the sweat from June's face)* Mmm, lovely!

Sandy: Can't we get some camel's milk to drink?

June: No, I tried milking the camel, but it got the hump!

Doug: We'll just have to save our energy.

Sandy: Yes, it's far too hot for digging.

June: I agree. You'd better put your shovels down.

Doug: *(Doug and Sandy are surprised but pleased)* You mean we don't have to dig today?

June: Of course you don't! You can use the rake, Doug, and Sandy can use the metal detector.

Sandy: What about you?

June: I'm going to have a long drink – I mean think! I'm going to have a long think about where we can get some water.

Doug: Come on then, I suppose we'd better get on with it. *(Doug hunts around, looking for something. Sandy uses the detector, which promptly beeps)*

Doug: You've found something!

Sandy: Yes – your rake!

Doug: Oh, thanks! I was looking for that! *(He picks up the rake, but the detector doesn't stop beeping)*

Sandy: It's still beeping. You know what that means, don't you?

Doug: Yes! It means you've got to take your boots off!

Sandy: It means we've found something! Perhaps June was right. Maybe we have found the Mighty GodSword!

Doug: Hang on: I'll rake it.

(Doug rakes and suddenly a jet of water spurts up from the ground. Doug and Sandy panic)

Doug: Oh no! I must have hit a water pipe!

Sandy: Hey! I'm getting soaked. Stop it, Doug!

(They try to block the flow, but that just makes it spurt out in different directions)

Doug: The water's being wasted! Quick, find something to catch it in!

Sandy: *(Handing him a clay pot)* Here – use this.

(Doug catches water in the pot, while Sandy manages to stop the leak)

Sandy: Phew! I could do with a drink after all that excitement!

Doug: Me too! I hope June's thought of a way to get some water.

Sandy: Give me that pot. *(He takes the pot from Doug and has a drink)*

Doug: Hold on – where did you get that pot from?

Sandy: You just gave it to me.

Doug: Oh yeah… but where did it come from before that?

Sandy: I found it in the sand. Hey – do you think it might be valuable? Perhaps it's an ancient wine jar? *(He drinks some more)*

Doug: Or maybe an ancient potty! *(Sandy pulls a face and hands the jar to Doug, who drinks eagerly)*

Sandy: See if there are any markings on the bottom of it.

(Doug turns it upside-down to check, thus pouring water all over himself! He doesn't seem to notice though)

Doug: I can't see any.

Sandy: We'll have to send it to the Professor then.

Doug: Do you think we should put some water in it, in case he's thirsty?

Sandy: No. Come on – let's show it to June.

(They both exit)

DRAMA (EPISODE 5)

PROPS YOU NEED FOR THIS EPISODE

- A 'bomb' (a large plastic drinks bottle, painted silver or black)
- A large Bible, preferably old and leather-bound (this is only to be used if you are not using the video)
- A piece of large, off-white cloth which is wrapped around the Bible

SCRIPT

(Doug, Sandy and June are digging)

June: Shhh!

Doug: What is it?

June: I think I can hear the telephone ringing.

Sandy: What telephone?

June: I'd better go and answer it. See you later!

Sandy: But June… *(June has already gone)* Doug, we haven't got a telephone. The nearest telephone is 200 miles away!

Doug: Wow! June must have really good hearing! Unlike me: I've got sand in my ears.

Sandy: I think you've got sand **between** your ears!

Doug: Yes! And between my toes, and down my back, and even in my pants! It's really itchy!

Sandy: I know what you mean, this sand gets everywhere!

Doug: Pardon?

Sandy: I said this sand gets everywhere!

Doug: I can't hear you because I've got sand in my ears. This sand gets everywhere!

Sandy: Come on, let's try to shake it out of our clothes.

(They both jump about and shake their arms and legs with very exaggerated movements. You could involve the children at this point, by getting them to stand up and join in. This could then lead into a 'workout' session)

Sandy: We'd better keep digging for the Mighty GodSword I suppose. I shouldn't think we'll see June for a while.

Doug: Not if she had to walk 200 miles to the telephone! Dig carefully, Sandy. This sand gets everywhere!

(They both begin to dig)

Doug: Oh! I've found something metal.

Sandy: Oh no! You've probably hit the water pipe again!

Doug: Sandy, you worry too much. It's not the water pipe at all.

Sandy: Phew! That's a relief! What is it then?

Doug: *(Holding it up)* It's a bomb!

(There follows a slapstick sequence. Sandy screams and that makes Doug jump and drop the bomb. Sandy catches it just in time, but then he trips and the bomb flies through the air. Doug catches it. They put it down very carefully, but then they drop a spade onto it. They run away (among the children) and take cover, but nothing happens.

At this point, they could involve the children, by making them all evacuate to the back, very carefully and quietly. Sandy and Doug remain at the back, with the children.

June enters, picks up the bomb, unscrews the cap, and has a drink. Then she replaces the cap and casually throws the bomb away)

June: I wonder where Doug and Sandy have gone. Oh well, if they're not here, I think I'll go and have another sleep. *(June exits)*

Doug: It must be safe. June didn't make it go pop.

Sandy: No, June made all the pop go. She drank the lot! Can't you tell the difference between a bomb and a bottle? Come on.

(Doug and Sandy return to the stage. The children can also move forward again)

Doug: You'd better go and pick up that bottle, Sandy. We mustn't be litterbugs.

Sandy: *(Scared)* Bugs! Where? I hate bugs!

Doug: Never mind about bugs; just pick it up.

Sandy: I can't, I've lost my bottle.

Doug: You've lost your bottle? Well, don't worry; there's a spare one over there.

Sandy: Oh, thanks. I'll go and fetch it. *(He goes to fetch the bottle)* Hey Doug! There's something else here. It's a bit of cloth…

(The following dialogue is only necessary if you are not using the video.) … and it's wrapped around something hard… it's a book, a big book. It's heavy, too.

Doug: Maybe it will have some information in it about the Mighty GodSword.

Sandy: Let's have a look. It seems to have lots of different sections. But they've got funny names. There's one called Genesis, but it's not about the pop group. And this one's got lots of words in it, even though it's called the book of Numbers. And what's this one, Job. I could do with a new job, then I might be able to get out of this desert!

Doug: I'm sure this is going to tell us where to find the Mighty GodSword. Although it's hard to know where exactly to look. There are just so many pages.

Sandy: Is June any good at reading? Have you ever seen her read any books?

Doug: No! But there's always a first time. But what about this cloth?
What's this for?

(Continue at this point if you are using the video)

Doug: What's this for?

Sandy: Let's go and find June, then we can send these/this to the Professor. Come on!

(*They exit, shouting excitedly to June as they go*)

DRAMA (EPISODE 6)

PROPS YOU NEED FOR THIS EPISODE

- A camp bed
- A rucksack or kit-bag
- A piece of paper, preferably stained beforehand with tea to make it look brown and old

SCRIPT

(*Enter Doug and Sandy*)

Sandy: What shall we do now that we've found the Mighty GodSword?

Doug: You mean the Mighty God's **Word**.

Sandy: Have you got sand in your ears again? I said the Mighty God's **Word**.

Doug: Oh no you didn't!

Sandy: Oh yes I did!

Doug: (*Involving the children*) Oh no you didn't!

Sandy: Did!

Doug: Didn't!

(*They continue bickering for a while. Enter June*)

June: What are you two arguing about? I thought you'd be happy now that we've found the Mighty GodSword.

Doug: You mean the Mighty God's **Word**.

Sandy: That's what she said.

Doug: It isn't!

Sandy: 'Tis!

Doug: 'Tisn't!

(*They bicker again*)

June: Stop it!

Sandy: (*Muttering*) He started it!

Doug: (*Also muttering*) Didn't!

June: Come on. We've got to pack up our things so that we can go home. I'll tidy the tent and you two pack up out here.

(*There follows a slapstick routine with Doug and Sandy. For example, Sandy tips sand out of a bag, but accidentally tips it on to Doug. Doug picks up a spade and puts it over his shoulder, narrowly missing Sandy's head*)

(*June comes out of the tent with a camp bed*)

June: This bed looks a bit wobbly to me. I think I'd better test it to make sure it's OK before I pack it away. *(She lies on the bed and promptly falls asleep)*

Sandy: There's another bed in the tent. Perhaps I'd better test that too.

Doug: No! I want to test it.

Sandy: No you're not, because I'm going to get there first. *(He runs into the tent, closely followed by Doug)*

Doug: *(From inside the tent)* Get off that bed!

Sandy: No!

Doug: Well move over then!

Sandy: No! *(Pause)* Ow! Get off!

Doug: Not until you get off the bed.

Sandy: Shan't!

Doug: Shall!

(They continue arguing from inside the tent. Then there is movement and there appears to be a fight going on. Finally the tent collapses on top of them)

June: *(Woken by the noise)* What was that? Hey you two, stop messing about and come and pack.

(They crawl out from underneath the tent. Sandy begins tidying. Doug starts to fill his rucksack with sand. June gets up and yawns and stretches in an exaggerated manner. Then she notices what Doug is doing)

June: Doug, why are you filling your bag with sand?

Sandy: I think he's making sandbags to protect him from that 'bomb' we found yesterday.

Doug: No I'm not! I just thought I'd take some sand for a souvenir!

June: Don't be silly, Doug! We haven't got enough room in our luggage for you to take sand home.

Doug: Yes we have; your rucksack's empty.

June: Yes, but… er… I need to keep it empty.

Sandy: Why?

June: Er… in case we find any more interesting things on our way home.

Sandy: But we're going on a plane for most of the journey! You won't find much interesting stuff on a plane.

Doug: That's true. Planes can be very plain.

June: Well, you never know. There might be a particularly interesting sick bag to add to my collection!

Doug: All right then, I'll empty out the sand. *(He does, and out comes a piece of paper too)*

Sandy: Hey! What's that? It looks like a letter!

June: It is a letter! You see? It's a good job my bag's empty, or we wouldn't be able to carry the letter to the camel-post station. *(She picks up her empty bag very easily and puts the letter inside. Then she acts as if the bag is very heavy)*

June: Come on then! I'll bring this heavy bag, and you just bring all the other equipment!

Sandy: *(As they exit)* I hate the desert. In fact, I never want to see sand ever again. When we get home, I'm just going to lie on the beach and do nothing all day!

TEACHING SCRIPTS – THE PROFESSOR

If you are using the **DESERT DETECTIVES VIDEO**, you may not need these scripts, because the video features the Professor too. But you might like to use the scripts in your leaders' training or preparation times, to give them an overview of the Bible story. And there is not a video episode for either of the two Sunday services, so you will want to use the scripts for these.

If you are not using the video, these scripts will enable the Professor to summarise the whole Bible story in seven parts. The Professor can be male or female, although for clarity the Professor is referred to as 'he' in these scripts. You may decide that the scripts are too long for younger children. There is an asterisk on each episode, except Episodes 3, 5 and 6, where you can make a break. If the location allows it, younger children can leave at this point.

The Professor should have a large Bible bookcase, containing 66 individual books representing the books of the Bible. The scripts can then be stuck inside the relevant books. Each different type of book should be a different colour, preferably to match the colours suggested on the children's expedition sheets:

LAW	(Genesis – Deuteronomy)	Red
HISTORY	(Joshua – Esther)	Yellow
WISDOM	(Job – Song of Songs)	Purple
PROPHECY	(Isaiah – Malachi)	Green
GOSPELS	(Matthew – John)	Blue
NT HISTORY	(Acts)	Yellow
LETTERS	(Romans – Jude)	Pink
NT PROPHECY	(Revelation)	Green

 Ask your church members to collect old telephone books and catalogues to make the Bible books, and make covers from coloured paper.

As the Professor reads the script, another leader should display pictures on an overhead projector to illustrate the different events. Your local Christian bookshop will have a selection of photocopiable clip art books to provide the necessary pictures. *How to cheat at visual aids* (SU) is particularly useful for this purpose.

Alternatively, the Professor could draw on a blackboard or similar as he speaks. Each script includes suggestions for pictures that can be sketched simply, but you will need to adapt these ideas to fit the resources you have available.

It is important to practise telling the story so that it sounds natural coming from your Professor's mouth. Each day there is one central story. Make sure that it has been clearly communicated.

SUNDAY 1 – GENESIS/THE BEGINNING

PROF'S PROPS

- The parcel or envelope from the drama (see page 20), containing:
  - sand
  - the Desert Detectives' letter (a copy of Prof's Post below)
- A copy of Prof's Prompts below, pasted into the front of Genesis in your Bible bookcase
- Pictures or OHP slides to illustrate some of the items. For example
  - creation – sun, moon, stars, plants, fish, birds, animals, people
  - Adam and Eve – tree and fruit
  - Noah – animals, ark, clouds, rainbow
  - Abraham – stars
  - Jacob/Israel and sons – family tree

PROF'S POST

(The Professor tips out the sand on to his desk, and reads the letter)

> Dear Professor,
>
> Having a lovely time. Wish you were here. The weather is hot and sunny.
>
> We haven't found the Mighty GodSword yet, but we did manage to dig up this. Can you tell us more about it, please? We'd like to know where it comes from and who made it.
>
> Thanks very much,
>
> From the Desert Detectives

(The Professor talks as he searches in the pile of sand) I wonder what they've sent me. It must be something quite delicate, because they've packed it in sand to keep it safe. It must be very small, too. Maybe even valuable. Hold on a minute! There's nothing here. Brilliant! I send the Desert Detectives thousands of miles to the desert in search of treasure, and they send me back some sand! And they want to know where it comes from and who made it! Well, I bet the answer is in my Bible bookshelf. Let's start at the beginning. The first book is called Genesis.

(He takes down Genesis and opens it at the beginning)

PROF'S PROMPTS

Genesis is all about beginnings. That's what the word 'genesis' means. In fact the very first words in the Bible are: 'In the beginning, God created the heavens and the earth.' Genesis tells us how God made the whole universe. That includes the world and everything in it, including us! God made light; the sky; the land, the sea, and plants; the sun, moon, and stars; fish and birds; animals and people. Then he had a rest!

So now we know where the sand came from. God made it! But let's see what else is in Genesis.

The people that God made were called Adam and Eve. God gave them a beautiful garden to live in. He said they could do whatever they liked, as long as they didn't eat the fruit from a special tree that was in the middle of the garden. But Adam and Eve disobeyed God and ate the fruit from the special tree. This made God sad and angry, and he sent Adam and Eve away from the beautiful garden.

Adam and Eve had children, but they disobeyed God too. Their oldest boy, Cain, killed his brother Abel just because he was jealous of him. God was angry with Cain and he sent Cain away too. In fact, Adam and Eve's descendants kept on disobeying God. This went on for hundreds of years, until it got so bad that God decided to wash all the bad things away and start again.

But one man, called Noah, still lived God's way and obeyed him. So God made sure that Noah and his family didn't get washed away too. God told Noah to build a big boat. Noah and his family got on board, and God sent lots of animals to get on too. God shut the door of the boat. Then he made it rain so hard, and for so long, that all the land was covered in deep water. But Noah, his family and the animals were safe in their boat. After the rain had stopped and the water had gone, God made a rainbow as a sign that he would never flood the world like that again.

Noah had lots of descendants and they lived in lots of different countries. Over the years, a lot of them even forgot about God!

But God chose one country to be the special place where his people would live. And he told a man called Abram to go there with his family and start it all off. God promised Abram that he would have more descendants than the stars in the sky or the grains of sand on the seashore. In fact, God gave him a new name: Abraham, which means father of many nations. Abraham wasn't sure how he would live up to his new name. He and his wife Sarah didn't have any children and Sarah was too old now to have a baby. But nothing is impossible for God and Sarah did have a baby boy.

They named him Isaac and when he grew up he married a beautiful woman called Rebekah. Isaac and Rebekah had twins, called Jacob and Esau. When Jacob and Esau grew up, they both got married and had children too. But Esau and his family moved away and lived in a different place.

God gave Jacob a new name, Israel. Israel had 12 sons. Their names were: Judah, Issachar, Zebulun, Reuben, Simeon, Gad, Naphtali, Asher, Dan, Levi, Benjamin and Joseph.

*But Israel's favourite son was Joseph and he gave him a special coat to wear. That made Joseph's brothers jealous. Joseph also had dreams about his brothers bowing down to him. That made his brothers jealous too, so they sold him as a slave.

Joseph was taken to Egypt. While he was there, the king of Egypt had dreams too. No one could tell the king what the dreams meant. But Joseph could. He told the king that a famine was coming, and he gave the king wise advice about storing grain to get ready for the famine. The king was so impressed that he gave Joseph a very high rank and put him in charge of the grain stores.

When the famine had begun, people from other countries heard that there was food in Egypt, so they came to Joseph to ask for help. One day Joseph's own brothers came, but they didn't recognise Joseph. They just saw a powerful ruler. So they bowed down to him, just like in Joseph's dream, and asked for help.

When Joseph told his brothers who he was, they were pleased to see him. And he was pleased to see them too. He invited all his brothers, and their dad, Israel, to come and live in Egypt with him. By then, all Joseph's brothers had children of their own, and some had grandchildren too. Joseph also had two sons, called Manasseh and Ephraim. Joseph's sons, as well as his brothers, were known as the children of Israel. Over the years their families grew bigger. They grew so big that they became tribes: the tribes of Israel.

And all those tribes were descended from Abraham, because Israel was Abraham's grandson. So God had kept his promise that Abraham would have more descendants than the grains of sand on the seashore.

(He picks up a handful of sand) I wonder how many grains of sand I've got here. Too many to count! But I've got lots to tell the Desert Detectives! Now, where did I put my writing paper?

DAY 1 – LAW BOOKS

PROF'S PROPS

- The parcel or envelope from the drama (see page 21), containing:
  - a piece of a stone slab (and lots of sand!)
  - the Desert Detectives' letter (a copy of Prof's Post below)
  - a soft clothes brush

- A copy of Prof's Prompts below, pasted into Exodus in your Bible bookcase
- Pictures or OHP slides to illustrate some of the items, for example:
  - pyramids
  - basket and bulrushes
  - plagues – frogs, flies, hailstones etc
  - pillars of cloud and fire
  - manna and rock with water coming out
  - Sinai – mountain, cloud, lightning
  - stone tablets
  - a copy of the Ten Commandments

PROF'S POST

(The Professor takes the stone piece from the parcel, and reads the letter)

> *Dear Professor,*
>
> *Having a lovely time. The weather is hot and sunny… again.*
>
> *We still haven't found the Mighty GodSword, but we found this interesting piece of stone with writing on it. It looks like it says something about a donut-covered donkey! Can you make any sense of it, please?*
>
> *Lots of love,*
>
> *From the Desert Detectives*

Donut-covered donkey? I haven't come across that phrase before. But the stone is a bit dusty. Perhaps if I clean it a bit… *(He dusts the stone with a soft brush)* That's better! Ah! It doesn't say, 'Donut' at all; it says, 'Do not'. I can't quite make out the next word, but this sounds to me like a rule or a law. Let's look for clues in the Law section of my Bible bookcase. These Law books have lots of rules and regulations in them, but they also tell the story of how those rules were made. Let's look at this one: it's called Exodus…

(He takes down Exodus and opens it)

PROF'S PROMPTS

Exodus starts about 400 years after Israel and his family went to live in Egypt with Joseph. There were thousands of people in Egypt who were descendants of Joseph's dad, Israel. So they were called the Israelites.

In fact, there were so many Israelites that the pharaoh (the king of Egypt) got scared of them. He tried to keep them in order by making them slaves and killing some of their sons. One woman hid her baby boy to save him from being killed. The pharaoh's daughter found the baby. But she was kind to him. She took him home and named him Moses.

But Moses wasn't an Egyptian; he was an Israelite, from the tribe of Levi. And when he grew up, God told him to speak to the pharaoh and tell him to set the Israelites free. But the pharaoh wouldn't listen to God's message, so God sent a series of plagues on Egypt to teach the pharaoh a lesson. First, the River Nile turned to blood. Then Egypt was infested with frogs, gnats and flies. After that, a disease killed some of the farm animals. Then the Egyptians got nasty boils, and there were hailstorms and swarms of locusts. Even when it went dark in the daytime, the pharaoh wouldn't let the Israelites go.

But when all the Egyptians' eldest sons died, then the pharaoh let them go. They had a special meal to celebrate and then they packed up all their belongings and left Egypt. God showed them the way to go. In the daytime he gave them a pillar of cloud to follow and at night a pillar of fire.

When the Israelites camped by the sea, the pharaoh changed his mind and came after them. They were trapped between the sea and the Egyptian army! But then God did an amazing thing. He turned back the sea and made a dry path through it for the Israelites to cross. When the Egyptian army chased them, the water came back and the Egyptian army was drowned.

After that the Israelites still had a long way to go across the desert. It took them a long time, but God looked after them. He gave them water to drink and every morning he gave them special food called manna. When they had nothing to drink, God told Moses to hit a rock with his stick. When he did, water came out of the rock.

Three months after the Israelites left Egypt, God met them on a mountain called Sinai. There was thunder and lightning and a cloud covered the mountain. There was a very loud trumpet blast and God came down in fire. The whole mountain shook; smoke covered it and the trumpet sound got louder and louder. God called Moses up the mountain, where he gave him a set of rules for the Israelites. God carved these on stone slabs and gave them to Moses to keep. There were lots of rules, about all sorts of things, but there were ten main ones. Here they are: *(This is the version taken from the CEV, with number 10 slightly amended)*

1 I AM THE LORD YOUR GOD, THE ONE WHO BROUGHT YOU OUT OF EGYPT WHERE YOU WERE SLAVES. DO NOT WORSHIP ANY GOD EXCEPT ME.

2 DON'T BOW DOWN AND WORSHIP IDOLS.

3 DO NOT MISUSE MY NAME.

4 REMEMBER THAT THE SABBATH DAY BELONGS TO ME. YOU HAVE SIX DAYS WHEN YOU CAN DO YOUR WORK, BUT THE SEVENTH DAY OF EACH WEEK BELONGS TO ME, YOUR GOD. NO ONE IS TO WORK ON THAT DAY.

5 RESPECT YOUR FATHER AND YOUR MOTHER, AND YOU WILL LIVE A LONG TIME IN THE LAND I AM GIVING YOU.

6 DO NOT MURDER.

7 BE FAITHFUL IN MARRIAGE.

8 DO NOT STEAL.

9 DO NOT TELL LIES ABOUT OTHERS.

10 DO NOT COVET ANYTHING THAT BELONGS TO SOMEONE ELSE. DON'T COVET ANYONE'S HOUSE, WIFE OR HUSBAND, SLAVES, OXEN, DONKEYS OR ANYTHING ELSE.

Ah! That's probably what the words on my piece of stone say. It doesn't say, 'Donut-covered', it says, 'Do not covet'. In other words, don't be jealous of what other people have. Maybe this stone is part of the Ten Commandments!

*But why did the stone slabs get broken? Let's read on…

Moses was with God on the mountain for a long time and the people didn't know what to do while he was away. So they decided to make their own god. They melted down their jewellery and made a golden calf to worship. When Moses saw it, he was so angry that he dropped the stone tablets he was holding and they broke. Moses destroyed the golden calf and told the people they should never worship idols. After that Moses had to go back up the mountain. God gave him some new stones. When Moses came down again, his face was shining and everybody knew that he had met with God.

These rules were so important that God told the Israelites how to make a special box to keep them in. The box is sometimes called the covenant box. God also gave them instructions to make a special temple-tent you could carry anywhere where they could put the covenant box when they camped. It was called the tabernacle. The people brought gifts to make furniture and equipment for the temple-tent. Moses' tribe, the tribe of Levi, became the priests and it was their job to look after the temple-tent and the box with the Ten Commandments in it. This was such an important job that the people from the tribe of Levi (the Levites) were set apart from the other twelve tribes and treated differently.

After a long time travelling in the desert, the Israelites came near to the land that God had promised to give them. It was called Canaan. Moses sent twelve spies into Canaan, one from each tribe. The spies found that it was a really good land with plenty of food, but they also saw strong walled cities and very big people. So when the spies reported back, ten of them said the land was too strong for the Israelites to conquer it. Only two of the spies said that they should trust God and go into the land. Their names were Caleb and Joshua.

Because the people didn't trust him, God made them wait before they could go into Canaan. But God was pleased with Caleb and Joshua, and when Moses died, Joshua became the new leader. Joshua was from the tribe of Ephraim.

DAY 2 – HISTORY BOOKS

PROF'S PROPS

- The parcel or envelope from the drama (see page 23), containing:
    - a ram's horn or trumpet (and lots of sand!)
    - the Desert Detectives' letter (a copy of Prof's Post below)
    - A copy of Prof's Prompts below, pasted into Joshua and Judges in your Bible bookcase

- Pictures or OHP slides to illustrate some of the items, for example:
    - walled city
    - trumpets
    - collapsed walls
    - clay jars
    - person with long hair
    - pillar

PROF'S POST

(The Professor takes the trumpet from the parcel, and reads the letter)

> *Dear Professor,*
>
> *Having a lovely time. The weather is still hot and sunny.*
>
> *No sign of the Mighty GodSword yet, but this ram's horn/trumpet might interest you. Perhaps you could make some notes on it for us!*
>
> *We are looking forward to your reply,*
>
> *From the Desert Detectives*

'Make some notes on it': very funny! *(He tries but only sand comes out)* Well, let's pick up the story where we left off, and see if we can find any mention of trumpets. We've finished the Law section of the Bible bookcase, so let's start at the beginning of the History section. The first book in this section is called Joshua, and it's all about what Joshua did after he took over as leader from Moses. *(He takes down Joshua and opens it)*

PROF'S PROMPTS

It was now time for the Israelites to enter Canaan, the land that God had promised them. The only trouble was that the River Jordan was in the way! And on the other side of the river there was a big walled city called Jericho.

Joshua sent two spies across the river to check out Jericho's defences. The spies got into Jericho, but the king found out that they were there and sent soldiers to catch them. A woman called Rahab hid the spies under some plants on top of her flat roof and the soldiers didn't find them. Because Rahab helped the spies, they promised that the Israelites wouldn't hurt Rahab and her family when they fought against the city. They told her to tie a piece of red rope on her window, so that the Israelites would know which one was her house and would leave it alone. Rahab let the spies escape out of her window and they went back to Joshua and the Israelites.

God told the priests to take the covenant box and carry it a little way into the river. As soon as they stepped into the river, it stopped flowing and there was a dry path through the river. The priests with the covenant box stood in the middle of the dry river bed until all the Israelites had crossed over.

Then God told the Israelites how to capture Jericho. God's instructions were a bit unusual, but the Israelites trusted him and did what he said. They marched slowly around Jericho once a day for six days. They took the covenant box with them, and seven priests marched in front of it, carrying trumpets. Ram's horns were used as trumpets in those days. Then on the seventh day, they marched around the city wall seven times, while the priests blew their trumpets. Finally, the priests gave a blast on their trumpets, everybody shouted…

…and Jericho's walls just fell down! Now the Israelites could easily go in and capture the city. But they kept their promise to Rahab. She and her family were kept safe.

After that, Joshua and the Israelites won more battles and captured more of the country. Some places still held out, but the Israelites captured most of the land and divided it up between the tribes.

(He picks up ram's horn/trumpet) I wonder if this is one of the trumpets they used. But maybe it's from a later time. Let's have a look at the next History book: Judges. *(Put Joshua book away and get out Judges)*

The people from Canaan were called the Canaanites and some of them worshipped a false god called Baal. Some of the Israelites started to worship Baal too, instead of the real God.

And every so often, other countries attacked the Israelites. When these things happened, God would appoint someone as a leader to sort things out. These leaders were called judges, but they weren't like court judges. They were more like battle chiefs.

One example is Gideon, from the tribe of Manasseh. God chose Gideon to destroy the altars to Baal and to fight a large army of invaders called the Midianites.

Gideon collected an army of 32,000 men, but God said it was too big! So Gideon said anyone who was afraid could go home. Only 10,000 men stayed, but God said there were still too many! When the men went to the water to drink, 300 of them scooped up water in their hands and all the rest knelt down to drink. God told Gideon to keep only the 300 men who hadn't knelt down!

Gideon gave each of them a trumpet and a large clay jar with a burning torch inside. After dark, they surrounded the Midianites' camp and waited for Gideon's signal. Then all at once they smashed their jars and held up their torches. They blew their trumpets and yelled. The Midianites panicked and in the dark they started fighting each other! That's how God helped Gideon to defeat the Midianites.

So maybe the Desert Detectives found a trumpet from that battle! I wonder!

But there was another country nearby, whose people were even more troublesome than the Midianites. They were called the Philistines. But God chose another judge to fight the Philistines. He was from the tribe of Dan and his name was Samson.

As a sign of his devotion to God, Samson never cut his hair. Because of that, God gave Samson amazing strength. Once, when a lion attacked him, Samson killed it with his bare hands! And another time he killed 1,000 Philistines, and his only weapon was a donkey's jawbone!

Samson married a woman called Delilah, but that was a silly thing to do because Delilah was a Philistine. Delilah tricked Samson into telling her the secret of his amazing strength. Then, when Samson was asleep, the Philistines shaved off his hair. When Samson lost his hair, he lost his strength too, and the Philistines captured him. They put Samson in prison, but while he was there, his hair started to grow and his strength grew too.

The Philistines didn't worship God; they worshipped a false god called Dagon. They brought Samson to Dagon's temple, where they had a big celebration because they had captured him. But Samson prayed to God and God gave him his strength back. Samson pushed hard on one of the pillars that held up the temple and he pushed it right over! That made the whole temple come crashing down on all the people inside. Samson was killed, but he killed a huge number of Philistine enemies too.

You can read more about this in Judges and in the other History books in the Bible.

DAY 3 – POETRY AND WISDOM BOOKS

PROF'S PROPS

- The parcel or envelope from the drama (see page 25), containing:
    - a nappy (and lots of sand!)
    - the Desert Detectives' letter (a copy of Prof's Post below)
- A copy of Prof's Prompts below, pasted into 1 Samuel, 2 Samuel and 1 Kings in your Bible bookcase
- Pictures or OHP slides to illustrate some of the items, for example:

– crown	– piece of cloth
– jar of oil	– bath
– harp	– baby
– sheep	– sword
– stones and sling	

PROF'S POST

(The Professor takes the letter from the parcel, and reads it)

Dear Professor,

Having a lovely time. The weather has changed! It's now hotter and sunnier!

We hope you have a nappy time investigating our latest find! We advise you to handle it very carefully.

Love from the Desert Detectives

They've made a spelling mistake here; they've written 'nappy' instead of 'happy'. Let's see what they've sent me. *(He takes out the nappy)* Urgh! It is a nappy! That's disgusting! I think I'll put it right over there, where I can't smell it!

Well, we didn't come across any nappies in the books we looked at yesterday, so let's go on to the next History book – the first book of Samuel. *(He takes down 1 Samuel and opens it)*

PROF'S PROMPTS

Samuel was another judge who didn't cut his hair. He wasn't super-strong like Samson, but he did manage to keep the Philistines under control. When Samuel grew old, he appointed his two sons to be judges after him. But his sons were dishonest and accepted bribes to give unfair decisions. So the people said that they wanted Samuel to appoint a king instead, just like all the other countries.

God sent a person called Saul, from the tribe of Benjamin, to be the king. Samuel anointed Saul with oil and made him king.

Saul was quite a good leader, but he didn't always do exactly what God told him to. Because of this, God said that future kings wouldn't be from Saul's family. Instead, God told Samuel to anoint a boy called David to be the future king. David was from the tribe of Judah.

Saul kept getting in a bad temper. So his men looked for someone who could play the harp to soothe Saul and calm him down. The person they found was David! Whenever Saul became angry, David would play his harp and then Saul would feel better.

In fact, David wrote lots of songs. You can read them in the Bible, in a book called Psalms. You might know the twenty-third psalm. It's all about how God is like a shepherd who looks after us. The book of Psalms is in the Wisdom section of my library. As well as psalms it contains poems and wise sayings too.

The Philistines had a champion called Goliath who was over three metres tall. None of the Israelite soldiers dared to fight Goliath, but David did. He knew that with God's help he could kill Goliath. He didn't even wear armour or take a sword. He just took his shepherd's stick, five stones and a sling. When Goliath stepped towards him, David hurled a stone at him with his sling. It hit Goliath on the head and cracked his skull. Goliath fell down dead.

After that, King Saul gave David a high rank in the army. But David became really popular and Saul was jealous. One day when David played his harp for Saul, Saul tried to kill David with a spear. But Saul's son Jonathan really liked David, even though he knew that David would be king instead of him. Jonathan used arrows to give a message to David to warn him to run away from Saul.

Saul and his men searched for David to catch him and kill him. One day Saul went into a cave. David was hiding at the back of the cave, but Saul didn't know. David could have killed Saul, but instead he just cut off a piece of Saul's cloak so that Saul would know that David was loyal to him.

Saul still searched for David after this, but he had to stop because the Philistines attacked again. Saul and Jonathan went to fight the Philistines, but they were both killed in the battle.

When David heard about this, he was really sad, even though that meant he would now be the king. In fact, he wrote a song about their deaths.

But this song isn't in Psalms. It's in 2 Samuel, which tells us all about what David did when he was king. Lets have a look... *(Put away 1 Samuel and get out 2 Samuel)*

One of the first things David did was capture an enemy city and make it his capital. The new capital city was called Jerusalem and David built his palace there. He also brought to Jerusalem the special covenant box that had the Ten Commandments in it.

But David did some bad things too. One day he accidentally saw a woman called Bathsheba having a bath. David fancied Bathsheba, but she was already married to a soldier called Uriah. So David made sure that Uriah was killed in a battle. Then David married Bathsheba. Afterwards, David wrote a psalm asking God to forgive him for what he had done. It's Psalm number 51.

Some time later, David and Bathsheba had a baby boy. His name was Solomon.

You never know, maybe this is Solomon's nappy! When Solomon grew up, he became the next king. The first book of Kings tells us what he did. *(Put away 2 Samuel and get out 1 Kings)*

For example, he built a temple in Jerusalem and moved the covenant box into it.

God said that he would give Solomon anything he asked for. Solomon could have asked for riches or a long life, but instead he asked for wisdom to rule wisely. God was pleased, so he gave Solomon not just wisdom, but a long life and riches as well!

One day two women came to see King Solomon. They discovered just how wise Solomon was. They had a baby with them, and they both claimed that the baby was theirs. Solomon had to decide whose baby it was. How would you have decided? Solomon ordered his guards to cut the baby in half with a sword, so that the women could have half each. One woman thought that was OK, but the other one begged him to give the baby boy to the other woman rather than kill him. Then Solomon knew that she was the baby's real mother, so he gave the baby to her. All his people were amazed at how wise he was. King Solomon became famous for his wisdom, and he wrote thousands of wise sayings.

You can read some of them in the book of Proverbs, which is another book in the Wisdom section of the Bible library.

DAY 4 – PROPHECY BOOKS

PROF'S PROPS

- The parcel or envelope from the drama (see page 27), containing:
  - a clay pot (and lots of sand!)
  - the Desert Detectives' letter (a copy of Prof's Post below)
- Copies of the relevant parts of Prof's Prompts below, pasted into 1 Kings and Jeremiah in your Bible bookcase
- Pictures or OHP slides to illustrate some of the items, for example:
  - rough map showing the divided kingdom
  - clay pot
  - broken pot
  - scroll
  - fire
  - well

PROF'S POST

(The Professor takes the letter from the parcel, and reads it)

> *Dear Professor,*
>
> *The weather is very, very hot and we are very, very thirsty. We haven't found pots of treasure, but we have found a pot! We just hope it gets to you in one piece!*
>
> *Love from the Desert Detectives*

I'm not sure where to look for clues about a clay pot. So let's take pot luck and look at another History book – 1 Kings. *(Get out 1 Kings)*

PROF'S PROMPTS

When King Solomon died, his son became king. But the ten tribes in the north decided that they wanted to be a separate country with their own king. So they chose a different king and they made a city called Samaria their capital. They called their country Israel.

The other two tribes were Benjamin and Judah. They kept Solomon's son Rehoboam as their king, and they kept Jerusalem as their capital city. Judah was a much bigger tribe than Benjamin, so they called their country Judah.

You can read about Israel and Judah, and all their different kings, in the History section of the Bible bookcase. There are two books called Kings and two called Chronicles.

A lot of the kings were bad and worshipped false gods like Baal. This was against the laws that God had given to Moses, so God gave some people messages to give to the kings and the people. They warned both countries that God would punish them if they kept disobeying him and worshipping false gods. The people who brought these messages were called prophets and most of them have Bible books of their own.

Here they are, in the Prophecy section of my Bible bookcase. *(He points out the Prophecy section)* So far, I've been reading the books more or less in order, but I won't be able to do that in the Prophecy section. That's because the Prophecy books are arranged in size order rather than date order. In other words, the biggest books come first.

In Israel, prophets called Amos, Hosea and Jonah all gave God's warnings. But the people wouldn't stop doing bad things, so God allowed a powerful country called Assyria to invade Israel. The people of Israel were taken away to Assyria and people from other countries came to live in Israel instead.

Some of the kings in Judah did listen to the prophets and turned back to God, so God kept Judah safe from the Assyrians. But other kings turned their backs on God and did evil things. So later on, God allowed another powerful country, Babylonia, to attack Judah to teach them a lesson. But God hadn't given up on his people. He used another prophet, Jeremiah, to give the people one last chance to turn back to him and be saved from the Babylonians.

There's a book called Jeremiah, which tells us all about it. Let's have a look. *(Put away 1 Kings and get out Jeremiah)*

God gave Jeremiah lots of signs to warn the people. For example, one day he told Jeremiah to go to the potter's shop. Jeremiah watched as the potter began to make a pot, but then changed his mind, squashed it and started again. God said he was going to punish Judah, but he would change his mind if the people started obeying him.

God told Jeremiah to buy a pot from the potter, then go out and smash it! God said he would smash Judah and Jerusalem if the people kept doing wrong. Perhaps it was like this pot *(He holds up the Desert Detectives pot.)*

Jeremiah got his servant, who was called Baruch, to write down all God's messages on a scroll. Jeremiah himself couldn't take the scroll to the king because the king hated him so much that he wanted him dead. Instead, one of the king's servants read to the king everything that Jeremiah had dictated. It was winter and cold so the king was sitting close to the fire. As one part of the scroll was read out, the king would take it, cut it into pieces and drop the pieces into the fire. He didn't want to hear God's message.

Jeremiah was put in prison and then he was thrown into an old well-shaft. He was rescued from the well, but he was still kept under guard after that.

*But Jeremiah was proved right, because the Babylonians did destroy Jerusalem and conquer Judah. The people of Judah were taken away to Babylon. Jeremiah wrote some sad poems when Jerusalem was destroyed. You can read them in the book of Lamentations, which is also in the Prophecy section of the Bible bookcase.

But God hadn't given up on his people. There were more prophets, even in Babylon. People like Daniel and Ezekiel were prophets. But this time they didn't bring warnings; they brought encouraging messages of hope. They said that one day God would bring his people back together and that there would be a special person who would save them.

They were right. The last few books of the History section tell us that the people did indeed return to Jerusalem, and they rebuilt the walls and the temple. But to find out about God's special person, we'll need to look at the second half of the Bible bookcase. It's called the New Agreement, or New Testament. We'll look at it tomorrow.

DAY 5 - GOSPELS

PROF'S PROPS

- The parcel or envelope from the drama (see page 29), containing:
  - a Bible (and lots of sand!)
  - the Desert Detectives' letter (a copy of Prof's Post below)
  - large off-white cloth

- A copy of Prof's Prompts below, pasted into the front of John in your Bible bookcase

- OHP slide or large piece of paper, with John 1:14 written at the top

- Pictures to put underneath the verse as the Professor speaks. For example:

– angel	– bread and wine
– star	– crown of thorns
– host of angels	– cross
– lightning	– empty tomb
– loaves and fish	

PROF'S POST

(The Professor takes the Bible from the parcel, and reads the letter that's with it)

> *Dear Professor,*
>
> *We think we have nearly found the Mighty GodSword. We hope you can make sense of this cloth and book. Reading it should keep you busy for days and days. Don't fall asleep!*
>
> *Love from the Desert Detectives*

(He holds the cloth in one hand rather gingerly and the Bible in the other) What is this? Why have they sent me a cloth? And what is this book?

(He flicks through the book, stopping at Hebrews) Hang on! Just listen to this! It's in a section called Hebrews. 'The Mighty God's Word is alive and active, sharper than a two-edged sword.' So it mentions a sword… perhaps it's the Mighty GodSword? But listen to this – Mighty God's Word, Mighty GodSword, Mighty God's Word, Mighty GodSword. So we've found it. It wasn't a Mighty GodSword we were looking for at all, but the Mighty God's Word. It wasn't a sword but a book. It is powerful because it's God's Word. This is the treasure the Desert Detectives have been looking for. *(Pauses for reflection, looks through the book again)*

That's interesting. The Mighty God's Word has got the same books in it as my Bible bookshelf! So I sent the Desert Detectives to find the Mighty God's Word, and I had it here all along! The Mighty God's Word is the Bible! All the different parts, including History, Wisdom, Law and Prophecy, tell us what God is like, and what he wants us to be like.

But hang on! Even with all that information from all those people and written down in all those books, people still kept getting things wrong! They disobeyed God's laws and ignored his prophets. But God never gave up. Instead, he made a new agreement with his people, and the second half of the Bible tells us all about it. In fact, it's called the New Agreement, or New Testament. God gave people his Word in a new and special way. Let's find out more from one of the New Testament books… *(He takes John's Gospel from his Bible bookcase, opens it at the beginning, and reads…)*

PROF'S PROMPTS

> 'The Word became a human being and lived here with us. We saw his true glory, the glory of the only Son of the Father. From him all the kindness and all the truth of God have come down to us.' *(John 1:14 (CEV))*

Hey! That's the **Desert Detectives** memory verse, all put together.

The Mighty God's Word isn't just a book; it's a real-life person! God didn't just *tell* people his Word; he *showed* them. God's Son, Jesus, came to live on earth, so that people could get to know him. They could watch what he did, and listen to the things he said. Some of the people who knew Jesus, or who'd heard a lot about him, wrote books about him. Their names were Matthew, Mark, Luke and John, and their books are called the Gospels.

Let's look again at what John says in his Gospel: 'The Word became a human being and lived here with us.'

Did you know that Jesus came into the world just like you did? He was born as a baby. Matthew and Luke tell us all about it in their Gospels. An angel came to visit a young woman called Mary and her future husband, Joseph. He told them that Mary was going to have God's baby! They were to name him Jesus, which means 'God saves'. When Jesus was born, God put a special star in the sky to show where Jesus was, and he sent *loads* of angels to tell some shepherds about him.

One day when Jesus was older, he went up a mountain to pray. Suddenly, his face looked different, and his clothes became as bright as a flash of lightning. Then a cloud surrounded them, and a voice from the cloud said, 'This is my Son, whom I have chosen. Listen to him.' John was there and perhaps he was remembering this when he wrote: 'We saw his true glory, the glory of the only Son of the Father.'

Or perhaps John remembered some of the miracles that Jesus did – things that only God could do.

Jesus showed God's glory by doing lots of amazing things. For example, once he fed over 5,000 people with just five loaves of bread and two fish. And another time he made a storm stop, just by telling it to! Jesus also made a lot of sick people better, which showed God's love and kindness as well as his glory. John wrote about that, too: 'From him all the kindness, and all the truth of God have come down to us.'

People learned about God by watching what Jesus did. But they also learned a lot from the stories Jesus told. Stories like the one about the sheep that got lost or the Samaritan man who rescued a man who was attacked by robbers. Jesus' stories always had lessons in them if you listened carefully. Stories like that are called parables and the Gospels are full of them.

But even though Jesus clearly showed God's glory and kindness and truth, not everyone liked him. Just as people before had rejected God's word in the law and the prophets, some people also rejected Jesus, the living Word. Even while the crowd was cheering Jesus as he rode into Jerusalem, his enemies were plotting to get rid of him.

In Jerusalem, Jesus and his friends ate the special Passover meal together. But Jesus said that in future, it wouldn't just remind them of God rescuing the people from Egypt: they would remember Jesus too. He said that the bread and wine would remind them of his body and his blood. Jesus' friends were puzzled. Was Jesus saying that he would save people, just like God had done?

They couldn't imagine how Jesus would do this, especially when after the meal Jesus' enemies turned up with an armed mob and took him away. His friends wanted to fight, but Jesus went with the soldiers peacefully.

Jesus' enemies falsely accused him of crimes against God and they told the Roman authorities that he deserved to be killed. When the Roman governor questioned Jesus, he realised that Jesus hadn't done anything wrong. But the governor was scared of the mob, so he decided to have Jesus killed anyway.

He handed Jesus over to his soldiers, who teased Jesus because people said he was a king. They put a purple robe on him and made a crown for him out of thorns. And they whipped him and spat on him. Then they nailed him onto a wooden cross and left him there to die. When Jesus died it went dark for three hours, even though it was midday.

Three days later Jesus' friend Mary went to cry at the tomb where Jesus had been buried. But when she got there the tomb was empty. All that was in the tomb were two cloths, one that had been wrapped round his head which was separated from the larger pile of cloths which had been round his body. Perhaps it was like this cloth here. *(He picks up the cloth that has been sent from the Desert Detectives)* Anyway, Mary thought someone had stolen Jesus' body, but then Jesus came and spoke to her! He was alive! He'd definitely been dead when they'd buried him. But now Jesus was alive again!

Later on, Jesus' friend Thomas saw him as well, and two other people met him walking down the road. In fact, at least 500 people saw Jesus after he became alive again.

After that, Jesus went up to heaven to be with God, but he told his followers that he would send his Holy Spirit to be with them.

SUNDAY 2 – ACTS AND LETTERS

PROF'S PROPS
- The parcel or envelope from the drama (see page 31), containing:
  - a piece of parchment (and lots of sand!)
  - the Desert Detectives' letter (a copy of Prof's Post below)
- A copy of Prof's Prompts below, pasted into the front of Acts in your Bible bookcase
- Pictures or OHP slides to illustrate some of the items, for example:
  - fire
  - stones
  - map
  - letters

PROF'S POST

(The Professor takes the letter from the parcel, and reads it)

> Dear Professor,
>
> We're coming home now, so this will be the last letter from us. But we know you like letters, so we're sending you a piece of parchment we found. We think it's part of a letter, but we're not sure because the writing is too faded to read. Hopefully you'll be able to find out more about it.
>
> Love from the Desert Detectives

I think this letter may have been written after Jesus rose again and went back to heaven. The book of Acts tells us about that time, so let's see if it gives us any clues about who might have written this letter. *(He gets out Acts and opens it at the beginning)*

PROF'S PROMPTS

One day, after Jesus had gone back to heaven, his followers were all together celebrating Pentecost. Pentecost was a sort of harvest festival that happened 50 days after Passover. Suddenly, a noise like a strong wind filled the whole house, and something like fire appeared over each person there. They were all filled with God's Holy Spirit. Peter went out and spoke to the crowd all about Jesus and 3,000 people became Jesus' followers that day. This was the beginning of God's worldwide Church.

Another man called Stephen also spoke powerfully about Jesus. But the religious leaders didn't like Stephen talking about Jesus. They made up lies about him, so that he was arrested and sentenced to death. A young man called Saul held their coats while they killed Stephen by throwing stones at him. In fact Saul decided to make it his mission to get rid of as many Christians as he could. But Jesus had a different mission for Saul to do.

As Saul travelled along the road, a bright light from heaven suddenly flashed around him, and a voice said, 'Saul, Saul! Why are you doing these things against me?' It was Jesus' voice! Saul became a believer and was baptised. Instead of trying to stop the Christians from talking about Jesus, he did it himself! So now the religious leaders tried to kill Saul too, but he escaped. Later on, Saul changed his name to Paul.

The good news about Jesus carried on spreading. At first, the believers only told other people who were connected with the tribes of Israel, but Jesus told Peter in a vision that the good news about Jesus was for everyone in the world to hear!

After that Paul travelled all over the place, visiting lots of different regions to tell people about Jesus. Later on, Paul went on another journey. He went back to many of the places he'd been to before, but he visited some new places too. And when he couldn't visit some places himself, he wrote letters to the people there.

Eventually, the religious leaders captured Paul. They asked the Romans to send Paul back to Jerusalem, because they secretly planned to kill him on the way. But Paul foiled their plan by asking to be sent to Rome instead. Paul was put in prison in Rome, but he still wrote lots of letters to the believers he had visited.

Lots of these letters are in the Bible bookcase. Paul wrote some letters to individual people, such as Timothy, and some to groups of people, such as Ephesians, Philippians, Galatians and Thessalonians.

Some of the other believers wrote letters too, such as James, John and Peter. Their letters are named after the people who wrote them, rather than the people who received them.

Later, John was captured too, and was sent to a faraway island. While John was there, he had a vision from God and he wrote down what he saw. It's the last book in the Bible and it's called Revelation, because God revealed things to John.

Most of the books in the New Testament are letters and they can help us to understand more about who Jesus was and about the things he did and said. Do you remember the bit that the I read out? 'The word of God is alive and active, sharper than a two-edged sword.' That's from one of the letters. It's a letter to the Hebrews – in other words, to people from the tribes of Israel. But as Peter found out, the good news about Jesus is not just for them, but for all of us. If you want to find out more, you know how: look in the Mighty God's Word!

PART 4
Desert Detectives day by day

Each day's programme contains the following elements.

AIMS

The main aims of the day's activities.

LEADERS' PREPARATION

This has two purposes: to ensure that the leaders are familiar with the topics and teaching for the day, and to provide a chance for the team to study the Bible for themselves, not just as teachers, but in a more personal, devotional way. This is not an optional extra!

BASE CAMP

This is the time when the children are all together for activities led from the front. It includes:

WORKOUT

The workout gives children a chance to stretch their muscles in a fun way. Include simple exercises such as stretching and running on the spot. Make some of these relevant to the **Desert Detectives** theme, such as riding a camel, or shaking their bodies to shake sand out of their clothes. Be aware of children with disabilities. For example, if you have a child in a wheelchair, include lots of hand actions. Set the workout to fast, lively music.

SINGING

Children enjoy singing and learning new songs, but don't try to teach them too many new ones in one week!

THE DESERT DETECTIVES CHALLENGE

This is a game for just two or three volunteers, but the 'spectators' can also be involved by being encouraged to cheer for one of the contestants. Again, fast music and a lively commentary will add to the atmosphere.

DRAMA

Following the adventures of Doug, Sandy and June as they search for the Mighty GodSword.

THE PROFESSOR/VIDEO

The Professor features in the *DESERT DETECTIVES VIDEO*, or you can use the scripts starting on page 33. Either way, the Professor gives an overview of a section of the Bible, so that the children understand that each Bible story is in fact part of one big story – God's involvement in his world. The Professor also focuses on one particular story, which then usually forms the basis of the interactive teaching in the expedition time and the expedition sheets. You may wish to present a combination of the video and the Professor's scripts.

MEMORY VERSE

John 1:14. This is taught in stages each day. It is only on Day 5 that its relevance to **Desert Detectives** is fully revealed. The following stages are suggested, using this version from the CEV:

1 The Word became a human being
2 and lived here with us.
3 We saw his true glory, the glory of the only Son of the Father.
4 From him all the kindness and all the truth of God have come down to us.
5 John 1:14.

 Missing words for each day can be filled in using games such as hangman. Alternatively, write each word on a piece of desert-shaped paper (palm tree, camel) or on an acetate, removing words one at a time.

POSTBOX

This enables children to bring in pictures, jokes and prayers etc to share with Desert Detectives.

TENT GROUPS

This is the time spent in small groups. It includes:

OASIS

This is the refreshment time.

CRAFT

Ideas are given for each of the three main crafts listed on page 16. If you prefer to make individual daily crafts, use one of the ideas from the 'museum artefacts' section.

EXPEDITION SHEETS

These have puzzles and activities to reinforce the teaching. There are two sheets for each day. One is broadly aimed at 5 to 7 year-olds, and the other at the 8 to 10s. But the ages are not shown on the sheets so tent-group leaders can use whichever sheet is best suited to the particular children in their tent. To complete the expedition sheets, Desert Detectives will need to use a Bible. See page 58 for ideas on using the Bible with children. Alternatively or in addition, you may choose to use the **DESERT DETECTIVES' NOTEBOOK** with 8 to 11 year-olds. See page 7 and the inside front cover for details.

Each day's sheet has pictures of the Bible books relevant to that day's theme. Children colour these, then cut them out and stick them on to their bookshelf sheet (shown on the next page). Over the course of Desert Detectives, they will build up a complete Bible bookshelf.

There is not an expedition sheet for the Sunday services, so the books for those days are printed below. Give each child a set, either on the Sunday or on Day 5, so that they can complete their bookshelf. Alternatively, stick them into the bookshelf before you photocopy it, so each child's sheet already has these books in it.

PRAYER

Talk with God in a small group, encouraging Desert Detectives to participate.

EXPEDITIONS

Some activities, such as games, quizzes and role-plays, are best done in groups of 30 to 50 children.

Include the expedition session wherever it is appropriate for your holiday club. The expeditions section gives ideas for interactive activities to help the children to relate to and understand the main Bible story each day.

SUNDAY SERVICES

There is material for two Sunday Services. A service before the week can introduce the theme to your church, and encourage them to pray for the week ahead. It is also helpful to consider Genesis separately from the rest of the Law books, although they could be considered together on Day 1 if necessary.

The two Sunday services are different from the other five days because they do not have activities for small groups and there is no video episode. If you are using a 'live' Professor use the scripts on pages 34 and 45. If not, these scripts could be adapted to form the basis of your talk or sermon.

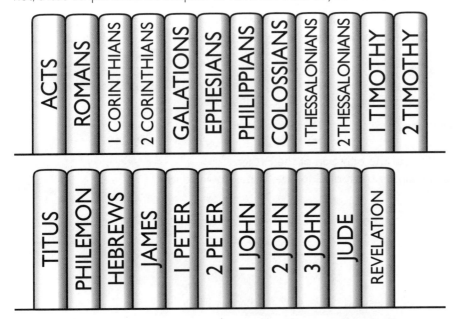

MY BIBLE BOOKCASE

SUNDAY 1 GENESIS

INTRODUCTION

The presenters should introduce themselves and the theme of **Desert Detectives**. This programme could be adapted to be the first day of a seven-day programme. Alternatively, this service can engage the whole church in what is planned and involve parents of children who will be coming all week. Decide how similar to a Sunday morning service you want this service to be.

SINGING

Teach the **Desert Detectives** song, and sing some general worship songs that your church is familiar with.

POSTBOX

Introduce the postbox and encourage children to bring things for the postbox tomorrow.

DRAMA (EPISODE A)

June goes off and Doug and Sandy start to dig. They shift a lot of sand but find nothing. But they fill a parcel with sand and tell June that the parcel contains a valuable find. The full script is on page 20.

THE DESERT DETECTIVES CHALLENGE

Preview tomorrow's challenge, perhaps with adult 'volunteers' rather than children.

WORKOUT

Encourage the whole congregation to join in if they are able.

PROFESSOR/SERMON

Look at how Genesis is the beginning of the world and of God's plan for the world. The script is on page 34.

SINGING

You may wish to include one or two of the following:

CREATION

'And God said'   kidsource 11
'God is good, God is great'   kidsource 73
'Who made the twinkling stars?'   kidsource 385
'Who put the colours in the rainbow?'   kidsource 386   Junior Praise 288
'Think of a world without any flowers'   Junior Praise 254

NOAH

'Mister Noah built an ark'   Junior Praise 167
'Oh, the Lord looked down'   Junior Praise 184

ABRAHAM

'Hold on to the promises of God'   kidsource 110 (omit verse 3)

PRAYER

Ask the church to pray for the week ahead. This is best done in small groups, if your church is used to praying in this way.

DAY 1 – LAW

AIMS FOR TODAY

1 To get an overview of the exodus

2 To see how it follows on from the events in Genesis

3 To learn about God's rules for his people in the Ten Commandments

4 To discover how God wants us to live in a right way, which pleases him

LEADERS' PREPARATION

The teaching today focuses on Exodus – Deuteronomy. These are the Law books. (Genesis is traditionally considered to be a Law book too, but there is so much in it that **Desert Detectives** covers Genesis separately in the introductory service.)

Exodus begins about 400 years after the events at the end of Genesis. But even so, it is part of the same story. The Israelites in Egypt were the descendants of Israel (Jacob) and his sons, who moved to Egypt to live with Joseph. But over time, they grew so numerous that they became a threat to the Egyptians, and the pharaohs who followed forgot Joseph. They made the Israelites slaves to keep them under control. But God hadn't forgotten them.

Exodus – Deuteronomy tells how God rescued his people from Egypt, and led them to the land he had promised them. On the way, God began to prepare them to be a nation. They were still arranged in separate tribes for administrative purposes, but God gave them a single leader, Moses, and a set of rules that would apply to all of them.

Read together Exodus 19:16–25, looking out for the evidence that God wanted to communicate with his people, but that he is also an awesome, holy God. Why was (and is) God concerned about how we live?

As you prepare together for the first day, ask God to give you a renewed understanding of his commandments and what they mean today. Ask him to help you to work as a team. Each team member should talk to the people either side of them to find out what their roles will be during the week and make a commitment to pray for them every day.

TENT GROUPS (15 MINUTES)

As this is the first day, you will need a number of assistants to help with the registration process. Children won't know where to go, so you'll need people who can take them to their tents and introduce them to their tent leaders. Leaders who don't have a group of their own should make themselves available for this. The tent leaders will then be able to stay with the children who have already arrived, and begin to get to know them. Allow an extra five minutes for this session on Day 1, as registration is likely to take longer than usual. During this session the children can make name badges or begin to decorate their tents.

BASE CAMP (35 MINUTES)

INTRODUCTION

Once all the children have arrived and settled, they assemble together at base camp. The presenters (in character if appropriate) introduce themselves and explain that they have been sent by the Professor to recruit some helpers to search for treasure. The children would make the ideal helpers, so they will become Desert Detectives for the week.

Say that there are some important things that all Desert Detectives should know! Tell the children where the toilets and exits are and explain any rules they need to follow. Add fun information too, such as a warning to stay away from orange and green snakes, or tips on what to feed the camels. This would also be a good time for a fire drill. Explain the procedure and then practise it. Again, link this to the theme in a fun way. For example, one of the presenters could mention sunburn, and another could react to the word 'burn' and evacuate everybody. Afterwards, explain that although that was a bit of fun, if the children hear the fire alarm again it will be serious and they should respond in the way they've just practised.

Explain that the treasure Desert Detectives are searching for is called the Mighty GodSword. The Professor has sent them to find this ancient treasure, because he says it has great value and power.

SINGING

Teach the children the **Desert Detectives** song, and perhaps other appropriate songs.

THE DESERT DETECTIVES CHALLENGE

Explain to the Desert Detectives that they only have one week to find the Mighty GodSword. Each day you'll be testing them to make sure they're up to the task. Today, you need two volunteers who are fast diggers.

Give each volunteer a teaspoon and a glass jar. They have one minute to shovel as much sand as they can into the jar with their spoons. Play lively music during the race and encourage the children to cheer for the volunteers. You could also add comments such as, 'Make sure you don't dig up any camel dung!' or, 'Watch out for scorpions!' The winner is the child with the most sand in their jar after the minute is up.

DRAMA (EPISODE 1)

June goes off to the toilet, leaving Doug and Sandy to dig. Sandy gets scared, especially when they dig up what seems to be part of an Egyptian mummy. June returns, and they realise it's not a bandage at all. It's June's toilet paper. They dig some more and find a piece of stone with writing on it. The writing appears to say, 'Donut-covered donkey.' The Desert Detectives don't understand this, so they send it to the Professor. The full script is on page 21.

WORKOUT

Children will have been sitting down for a while. They need to join in with the exercises. Explain that this will be a daily routine, because it's important for Desert Detectives to be fit and strong.

POSTBOX

Introduce the postbox. If you have already introduced it in the Sunday service, see if the children have put anything in it. Encourage children to bring in pictures, jokes and prayers to put in it.

THE PROFESSOR/VIDEO

The Professor cleans the stone the Desert Detectives sent him and realises that it says 'do not' rather than 'donut'. This seems like a rule, so he refers to the Law section in his Bible bookcase. He gives an overview of Exodus – Deuteronomy, emphasising that although there is a narrative story (mainly about a journey), much of the content is rules and laws. He refers in particular to the Ten Commandments, and realises that the piece of stone actually says, 'do not covet… donkey'. The full script is on page 36.

The video recreates the barren desert where God met with his people and gave them the law.

EXPEDITIONS

Write out each of the Ten Commandments on a separate piece of card. You'll need one for each tent, so you may need to omit or duplicate some commandments, depending on the size of your expedition. Each tent should devise a short sketch to illustrate their commandment, which is either being followed or being broken. Each tent acts out their sketch to the rest of the expedition, who have to guess which commandment it is.

Don't be afraid to include 'Do not commit adultery', particularly with older children. But do provide some guidance and supervision to make sure that the children don't get carried away in their role-play! 'Do not murder' should also be supervised, as over-zealous acting can sometimes be a bit rough.

TENT GROUPS (40 MINUTES)

OASIS

Refreshments

CRAFT

CRAFT 1: MUSEUM ARTEFACTS

Ideas could include: fragments of carved stone (made from clay); pyramid model (made from card); Egyptian hieroglyphics or paintings; papyrus (white paper stained with cold tea to make it brown and crinkly); Moses' basket (woven from raffia); burning bush model (branch with tissue-paper flames); a staff turning into a snake (use clay or Plasticene); plague pictures or models; Passover meal items; manna (or an explanation that manna cannot be displayed as it does not keep overnight!); stone tablets (made from clay); models of the tabernacle and covenant box (made from card, straws, cloth etc.); spies' reports.

CRAFT 2: BIBLE BOOKCASE

Each child should make the bookcase, and the first five books.

CRAFT 3: FRIEZE PICTURES

Each tent could choose one of the following to make into a picture: baby Moses; Moses and the burning bush; the plagues in Egypt; the pillars of cloud and fire; crossing the sea; collecting the manna; Mount Sinai; the Ten Commandments; the golden calf; the covenant box; the temple-tent.

EXPEDITION SHEETS

A maze reminds the children of the Israelites' journey from Egypt to Sinai, through the Red Sea.

There is also a puzzle about the Ten Commandments.

It is an opportunity to talk about rules and that God wanted us to have them because he loves us.

BASE CAMP (20 MINUTES)

SINGING

As well as the general songs, choose one or two that relate to today's story.

MEMORY VERSE

Teach the children the first line of the memory verse from John 1:14. See page 47.

POSTBOX

If there wasn't much in the postbox in the first base camp session, see if the children have put anything in it in the meantime. Remind them to bring things for the postbox tomorrow.

TENT GROUPS (10 MINUTES)

The children return to their tents to be collected. While they are waiting, they can decorate the tent, finish their expedition sheets or crafts, work on their notebooks, or prepare items for the postbox.

HAVE YOU THOUGHT ABOUT…?
WHERE CHILDREN ARE COMING FROM

A child's world is very different from what it was even five years ago. Children who come from stable family backgrounds and/or have a knowledge of the Bible will be in the minority. In the weeks before **Desert Detectives** watch children's television programmes, browse through the children's comics and magazines in the newsagent, talk with children about their experiences of school, friendships, computer games and leisure. Listen out for signs of a low self-image, uncertainties, the importance of relationships and a sense of their rights.

Much of what we introduce at **Desert Detectives** will be brand new. A personal God who wants a relationship with people could seem strange, especially if he makes it clear he wants us to live in a way that pleases him. To grasp that God loves us whatever we are like and wants to forgive us could be amazing news. Each day, challenge yourself to represent the truths in **Desert Detectives** in a way that is 100% appropriate for children living in the twenty-first century.

DAY 1 THE LAW

Find Moses' way from Egypt, through the sea, to Mount Sinai.

Moses was so cross when he came down the mountain that he smashed the Ten Commandments. Look at Exodus 32:19 to see why. Can you fit the pieces back together by matching up the missing words? You could do this as a group. Exodus 20:1-17 will help you.

OTHER GODS ANY
DO NOT BOW DOWN
DO NOT MISUSE
KEEP THE SEVENTH
AND MOTHER FATHER

DO NOT
IN MARRIAGE
DO NOT
LIES ABOUT
OTHERS
DO NOT COVET

DO NOT TELL
WORSHIP IDOLS AND
DAY HOLY
DO NOT WORSHIP
RESPECT YOUR
STEAL
GOD'S NAME
MURDER
BE FAITHFUL
SOMEONE ELSE'S THINGS

FACTFILE

• The name 'Moses' sounds in Hebrew like 'pulled out'. That's because Moses was pulled out of the water by Pharaoh's daughter.

• Moses was over 80 when he climbed up Mount Sinai to receive the Ten Commandments.

Think hard! Talk about the rules you have at **Desert Detectives**. Then talk about the reasons why you might steal or tell lies.

Ask God to help you keep his commandments, including the ones about not telling lies or stealing.

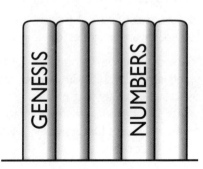
Talk with God

BIBLE BOOKCASE

– Fill in the missing books.
– Colour these books red.
– Cut them out.
– Stick them into the Law section of your Bible bookcase.

GENESIS   NUMBERS

DAY 1 THE LAW

Find Moses' way from Egypt, through the sea, to Mount Sinai.

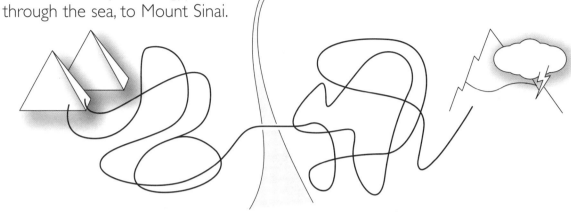

Look up two of God's commandments in Exodus 20:15,16. In the tablet of stone draw someone who is not keeping the commandment about stealing.

God gave his people the commandments because he wants us to...

Take the first letter of each picture to find the answer.

 Talk with God Ask God to help you obey his commandments, about not stealing and not lying.

 Think hard! Why do you have rules in **Desert Detectives**? Ask your tent leader about any of the Ten Commandments you don't understand.

BIBLE BOOKCASE

- Colour these books red.
- Cut them out.
- Stick them into the Law section of your Bible bookcase.

GENESIS EXODUS LEVITICUS NUMBERS DEUTERONOMY

Law

DAY 2 - HISTORY

AIMS FOR TODAY

1 To gain an overview of the period after the exodus, when the people settled in Canaan, but did not yet have a king

2 To learn how God helped his people to defeat Jericho

3 To see where the Judges fit into the overall story

4 To discover how God helps us to do the right thing and obey him, even when it may not seem to make sense

LEADERS' PREPARATION

The History section in the Bible includes Joshua – Esther. Between them these books cover several hundred years. But **Desert Detectives** only covers Joshua and Judges today. The rest of the History section is referred to later on, in connection with the Wisdom and Prophecy books.

Joshua tells how the Israelites occupied the promised land of Canaan. And Judges deals with the time before they had a king, when there were various rulers called judges, who were appointed at particular times to deal with specific threats from local powers. (Ruth deals with events during this period too, but it is not referred to in **Desert Detectives**.) This was a period of great instability. Various surrounding countries posed a threat, as did the Canaanites themselves, who hadn't been completely subdued. Even though the Israelites resisted attack, they were constantly subjected to the temptation to make life easy for themselves by adopting and worshipping the gods of their neighbours.

Read Judges 2:16–19, looking out for the two sides of the drama. God wanted his people to be safe but they chose to disobey him. What does this account tell you about God and his people?

As you prepare for **Desert Detectives** today and this week, ask God to help you to resist the temptation to make things easier by adapting his word to fit the values and beliefs of modern society. And ask him for strength to persevere with difficult children or situations. In small groups, pray for particular children by name.

TENT GROUPS (10 MINUTES)

When the children have registered they go straight to their tents. They can finish off some of yesterday's activities, or continue to decorate their tents. While this is going on, tent leaders should be getting to know their groups. Talk about what they enjoyed at **Desert Detectives** yesterday. But also allow them to talk about anything that interests them. Remember, the primary aim as the children arrive is to make them welcome and get to know them better.

BASE CAMP (40 MINUTES)

SINGING

Sing the **Desert Detectives** song and some of the general songs. Include one or two of the songs from yesterday to remind children of the story so far.

DRAMA (EPISODE 2)

The Desert Detectives use a metal detector, but it only beeps when Doug uses it, and even then they don't find any treasure. They eventually realise that Doug's steel toecaps are setting off the metal detector. Doug takes his boots off, but the sand is too hot for his bare feet, so he goes into the tent. When Doug has gone, Sandy and June find an old trumpet. The full script is on page 23.

WORKOUT

Some lively trumpet music would be good for this today. Include actions such as sweeping with a metal detector or dancing on the hot sand.

THE DESERT DETECTIVES CHALLENGE

Remind the children of yesterday's stories with a pyramid-building race. You'll need two volunteers and two packs of playing cards. The volunteers have one minute to build a pyramid making the cards into triangular shapes. The winner will be the person with the highest pyramid.

THE PROFESSOR/VIDEO

There are three parts to the Professor's explanation today.

1 The story of Joshua and Jericho

2 The story of Gideon

3 The story of Samson

The main story is the defeat of Jericho, but Gideon and Samson are included because many children will have heard of them. It's good to put their stories into context. Referring to two different judges helps to convey the idea that the judges dealt with different, local enemies. The full script is on page 38.

In the video, the children will be able to identify with the sound that caused the walls of Jericho to collapse. They will also begin to see how the sections of the Bible fit together.

EXPEDITIONS

Desert Detectives build a city from cardboard boxes, and then march around it acting out the story. They can make soldiers' or priests' breastplates to wear and trumpets to blow. Priests should carry a mock-up of the covenant box. The children should march around once for each of the first six days. They circle the city seven times for the seventh day, before shouting and blowing their trumpets. At this point, the walls should fall down!

 One way to make the walls fall down is to have a team member sitting inside the 'city'. She can then push the walls down at the appropriate moment.

TENT GROUPS (40 MINUTES)

Remember, this is the time to deepen relationships with the children, talking about what matters to them.

OASIS

Refreshments.

CRAFT

CRAFT 1: MUSEUM ARTEFACTS

Ideas could include Rahab's rope (made from strips of red cloth); rubble; trumpets (card cones), with a suitable handle attached; swords, shields and armour (made from card and gold/silver foil).

CRAFT 2: BIBLE BOOKCASE

Children add the 12 History books: Joshua to Esther.

CRAFT 3: FRIEZE PICTURES

Each tent could choose one of the following to make into a picture: the people crossing the River Jordan; Rahab hiding the spies; marching around Jericho; Jericho in ruins; Gideon at night with jars and torches; Samson with long hair; Samson with short hair.

EXPEDITION SHEETS

Today, 5 to 7 year-olds and 8 to 11 year-olds have similar expedition sheets. Make sure that you have enough Bibles or copies of the Bible passage for each child. Tent leaders should be prepared for a discussion about times when it is difficult to trust in God and obey him, however difficult it may seem.

BASE CAMP (20 MINUTES)

SINGING

Sing the songs you learnt yesterday and maybe introduce one that relates to today's story.

MEMORY VERSE

Recap the first line of the memory verse from John 1:14, and teach the children the second line. See page 47.

POSTBOX

By now, there should be plenty of items in the postbox. Only show the best ones, but display all of the items later on so that all the children's input is valued.

TENT GROUPS (40 MINUTES)

Children go back to their tents to finish off expedition sheets, crafts etc until children are collected.

HAVE YOU THOUGHT ABOUT…?
USING THE BIBLE WITH CHILDREN

As a result of **Desert Detectives** we want children to understand the fact that the Bible is God's message to us today and is accessible to people of all ages. So it is important that the times when you read the Bible with children are enjoyable and make sense!

We don't want children simply to read the Bible in order to answer our questions. We want to ask questions to stimulate their curiosity and expectation of meeting God as they read the Bible.

Make sure the Bible version you use is child-friendly, such as the CEV, Good News, NirV (New Light) or International Children's Version - and does not look tatty. You could copy out the relevant verses on to paper or an acetate. Ask a confident child to read and think of ways to engage children's thoughts as the verses are read. For example, on Day 1, if the children know they are going to act out a commandment, they will need to listen carefully to be able to choose which one to do. Or children can look out for or underline certain words.

Remember that many children find reading difficult and reading such a big book may be intimidating. With younger children you may just want to read out part of the Bible, inviting them to listen out for a key word. You may need to explain about chapters and verses and where to find each book. Refer to page numbers as well as Bible books.

Remember that you are a role model in the way you use the Bible. The children will notice if you take the Bible seriously and respectfully. They will pick up from you an expectation that God speaks to us as we read his Word. If you want to think more about this, get a copy of *The Adventure Begins* (SU) by Terry Clutterham. It will stimulate your thinking.

Be prepared to recommend a Bible-reading guide to follow up **Desert Detectives**. See the inside front cover for details of what is available for which age groups.

DAY 2 HISTORY

Read Joshua 6:1-5 together. What do you think the woman on the walls and the soldier might be thinking? Fill in the thought bubbles and add any missing details.

Read Joshua 6:20. Draw the expressions of the people as the walls fell down. What do you think they said?

 In your tent, talk about any times or places where you need to trust in God, or to do what he says. Ask God to help you to do what he is asking.

FACTFILE

• The first Old Testament History book is the book of Joshua which begins with the story of Joshua in 1200 BC.

• The History books end with the story of Esther, a Jewess who married a Persian king, 700 years later.

BIBLE BOOKCASE

- Fill in the missing books.
- Colour these books yellow.
- Cut them out.

- Stick them into the History section of your Bible bookcase.

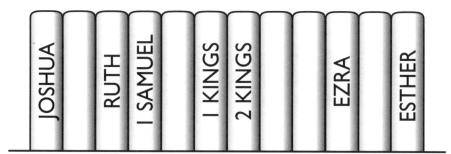

JOSHUA | RUTH | 1 SAMUEL | 1 KINGS | 2 KINGS | EZRA | ESTHER

DAY 2 HISTORY

Can you spot ten differences in these two pictures of the men marching around Jericho?

Read Joshua 6:20. Draw the expressions of the people as the walls fell down. What do you think they said?

Think hard! In your tent, talk about any times or places where you need to trust in God, or to do what he says. Ask God to help you to do what he is asking.

Talk with God

BIBLE BOOKCASE

– Colour these books yellow.

– Cut them out.

– Stick them into the History section of your Bible bookcase.

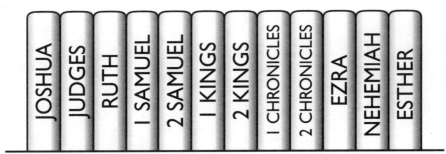

JOSHUA · JUDGES · RUTH · 1 SAMUEL · 2 SAMUEL · 1 KINGS · 2 KINGS · 1 CHRONICLES · 2 CHRONICLES · EZRA · NEHEMIAH · ESTHER

History

DAY 3 – WISDOM

AIMS FOR TODAY

1 To learn that after the Judges, there were some kings who united all the tribes into one nation

2 To look at how King Solomon showed wisdom

3 To find out that the Bible contains poetry and wise proverbs as well as rules and stories

4 To think about what true wisdom means. God wants us to know him and live in a way that pleases him

LEADERS' PREPARATION

The Wisdom books of the Bible are traditionally Job, Psalms, Proverbs, Ecclesiastes and Song of Songs. Some of these are poetry and songs, but **Desert Detectives** concentrates mostly on wisdom. Solomon wrote much of this, so this is an opportunity to continue the historical story by looking at the first few kings of Israel.

Wisdom is a bit of an abstract concept, so **Desert Detectives** uses a story to illustrate it. Team members should be familiar with the story in 1 Kings 3:16–28.

But as you prepare together, read Proverbs 9:10.

> Respect and obey the Lord! This is the beginning of wisdom. To have understanding, you must know the Holy God. (CEV)

Talk about what the children will understand about the term 'wisdom'. How does the Bible's view differ? Then read Proverbs 3:5–7. Ask God to give you true wisdom and to guide you as you help the children to 'know the Holy God'.

TENT GROUPS (10 MINUTES)

As the children arrive, they go to their tents to chat and finish off items from Days 1 and 2.

BASE CAMP (40 MINUTES)

DRAMA (EPISODE 3)

The Desert Detectives get a fright when someone picks up a snake instead of a rake. But it turns out to be June's pet snake, so they carry on digging. They find a smelly nappy, which they're only too pleased to send off quickly to the Professor. The full script is on page 25.

SINGING

Sing the **Desert Detectives** song, and some of the other songs from the last couple of days.

WORKOUT

Include some actions related to wrestling with a snake or changing a nappy.

THE DESERT DETECTIVES CHALLENGE

Two volunteers each have one minute to put a fabric nappy on a doll. The winner is the child with the neatest nappy.

THE PROFESSOR/VIDEO

The Professor picks up the story from yesterday, explaining how the people demanded a king. He talks about how Saul disobeyed God and David was anointed in his place. He tells the story of David and Goliath and mentions that David wrote a number of psalms. David's son Solomon became king after him and he asked God for wisdom. The Professor tells the story of Solomon and the two women with the baby. Finally, he refers to Solomon's wise sayings in Proverbs. The full script is on page 40.

The video contains a striking re-enactment of the dilemma Solomon faced. The Professor thinks he is gettng closer to the Mighty GodSword, but his hopes are dashed.

EXPEDITIONS

Each tent group needs a pencil and some paper. Prepare a list of items from Proverbs 3:13–26 that relate to wisdom, for example: gold; jewels; a tree; the sea; rain clouds; someone sleeping; storms.

One child from each tent group is shown the first item on the list. They run back to their tent and draw it as quickly as they can. The child drawing is not allowed to talk about or mime the item; he or she must only draw it. When someone guesses the item he or she draws the next one, and so on. The first tent to guess all the items wins.

After the game, read out the passage to show what the items have in common. Talk about wisdom. God is the source of all wisdom. After all, he created heaven and earth (verse 19). A wise person is someone who wants to know God so that they can live in a way that pleases God. That is worth far more than silver or jewels (verses 14, 15). You could interview a team member about how they know God and have become wise. Be practical about what it means to have a relationship with God.

TENT GROUPS (40 MINUTES)

OASIS

Refreshments

CRAFT IDEAS
CRAFT 1: MUSEUM ARTEFACTS

Ideas could include:

SAUL AND DAVID

Sheep (made from cotton wool); harp (made from string and card); sling and stones; anointing oil (a decorated bottle); crown (made from gold card); life-sized (3m) Goliath cut-out; Goliath's armour and sword.

SOLOMON

Temple model (made from boxes); Solomon's riches and jewels (made from foil and coloured cellophane).

GENERAL

Psalms and proverbs written out and illustrated.

CRAFT 2: BIBLE BOOKCASE

Children add five books: Job, Psalms, Proverbs, Ecclesiastes and Song of Songs. You may need to finish off the History books from yesterday.

CRAFT 3: FRIEZE PICTURES

Each tent could choose one of the following to make into a picture: Saul anointed king; David playing the harp; David the shepherd; David and Goliath; Solomon and the baby; Solomon's temple; Solomon's riches.

EXPEDITION SHEETS

The sheets for the two age groups are quite different. Solomon asked God for wisdom, which he then demonstrated in practice. Tent leaders should aim to talk about their own relationship with God and what it means to be wise. Make sure that you have enough Bibles or copies of the Bible verses for each child to be able to engage with the Bible for themselves.

BASE CAMP (20 MINUTES)

SINGING

The singing time is an opportunity to emphasise the other aspect of the Wisdom literature: the songs and poems. Sing some general praise songs too.

MEMORY VERSE

Recap the first two lines of the memory verse from John 1:14, and teach the children the next line. See page 47.

POSTBOX

TENT GROUPS (10 MINUTES)

Children return to their tents to finish off today's activities and to wait to be collected.

HAVE YOU THOUGHT ABOUT…?

WORKING WITH CHILDREN FROM OTHER FAITHS

PRINCIPLES TO WORK FROM

— We will not criticise, ridicule or belittle other religions.

— We will not tell the children what their faith says or define it by what some of its adherents do.

— We will not ask children to say, sing or pray things that they do not believe or that compromise their own faith.

— We will respect the faith of the children.

— We will value and acknowledge the children's culture.

— We will use music, artwork and methods that are culturally appropriate.

— We will be open and honest in our presentation of the Christian faith.

— We will be open and honest about the content of our work with parents and other significant adults.

— We will seek to build long-term friendships that are genuine and not dependent upon conversion.

— Where children show a genuine interest in the Christian faith, we will encourage them but be open and honest about the consequences. We will never encourage them to make decisions that could put them in danger.

PRACTICAL CONSIDERATIONS

— Many Asian communities (of all faiths, including Christian) are uncomfortable with bodily contact especially between boys and girls. Think about your games.

— Asian girls may prefer to be in single-sexed groups. Make allowance for this.

— Be culturally sensitive about the food you offer – eg no pork products (including gelatine) for Muslims, some Hindus don't eat eggs. Include a choice of snacks from various cultures.

— Be open about what goes on in **Desert Detectives**. Never suggest children keep things a secret.

— Acknowledge that children from other faith backgrounds have some understanding about the nature and person of God. Don't assume they know nothing or that what they know is wrong.

— Asking children to change faith is not only dangerous but inappropriate when it could mean exclusion from the family or even death.

DAY 3 WISDOM

FACTFILE
on King Solomon

• He wrote down thousands of proverbs and songs.

• He made the Kingdom of Israel very large, strong and powerful.

• He became very rich and welcomed foreign kings and queens as visitors.

• He had lots of wives!

Think hard! In your tent talk about what it means to be wise. How could you be wise in these situations?

Read 1 Kings 3:16-28 and answer these questions.

1 Who needed advice about a baby? (verse 16)

2 Who did they ask for help? (verse 16)

3 What weapon did the king ask for? (verse 24)

4 If this weapon was used, the baby would be
_ _ _ _ (verse 26)

5 At the end, Solomon knew who was the real
_ _ _ _ _ _ (verse 27)

6 Everyone was _____ at Solomon's wisdom.
(verse 28)

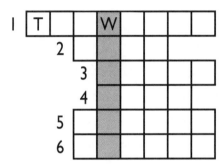

The word in the shaded boxes was the gift that Solomon wanted God to give him. He used it to help others, to be a good king and to please God. He wrote down many wise sayings which are included in the Wisdom books in the Bible. Look one of them up in Proverbs 3:5. Can you put that in your own words?

Read Proverbs 1:1. Who wrote these proverbs?

_ _ _ _ _ _ _ _ _ _ _

 Talk with God Pray together to ask God to give you wisdom, so that you'll know what's the right thing to do that pleases God.

BIBLE BOOKCASE

– Fill in the missing books.

– Colour these books purple.

– Cut them out.

– Stick them into the Wisdom section of your Bible bookcase.

JOB PSALMS ECCLESIASTES

DAY 3 WISDOM

Both of these women say the baby belongs to them. Read 1 Kings 3:16-28, then work out which of the mothers is the real mother.

No! Don't hurt the baby! Give it to her instead.

Half each? That's a good idea.

King Solomon asked God to make him wise. He wrote down many wise sayings. Look one of them up in Proverbs 3:5. Can you add the missing letters?

W_th _ll
y_ _r h_ _rt
y_ _ m_st
tr_st th_
L_rd.

How would you be wise in these two situations?

 Think hard!

Pray together to ask God to help you do what is right.

 Talk with God

BIBLE BOOKCASE

- Colour these books purple.
- Cut them out.
- Stick them into the Wisdom section of your Bible bookcase.

JOB PSALMS PROVERBS ECCLESIASTES S OF SONGS

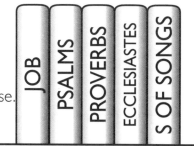

DAY 4 - PROPHECY

AIMS FOR TODAY

1 To discover that the kingdom was split in two, but both parts disobeyed God
2 To learn about the role of the prophets to bring God's warnings as well as promises
3 To learn that the people of Judah were exiled, but other prophets brought messages of hope for future salvation
4 To discover that God was and is committed to his people. He calls us to obey him

LEADERS' PREPARATION

Today's theme is Prophecy, looking particularly at the prophet Jeremiah. Jeremiah brought God's message, but the people wouldn't listen to him. Jeremiah became despondent.

Read Jeremiah 33:1–13. Imagine how desperate things are for the people in Jerusalem, and for Jeremiah in particular. Jeremiah's messages from God have been constantly ignored or rejected. What hope does God give Jeremiah? What aspects of God's character will become clear today?

Perhaps some of your team will be feeling despondent. They may have a difficult group, and feel that despite all their efforts, their message just isn't getting through. They may even be right, but of course we never know what effect our efforts will have in the future. Like Jeremiah, we must persevere and trust that God is in control. Pray for one another in small groups.

Finish on a positive note by encouraging team members to share any good experiences they have had.

TENT GROUPS (10 MINUTES)

You should know the children quite well by now, so the emphasis might be more on conversation rather than specific activities.

BASE CAMP (40 MINUTES)

DRAMA (EPISODE 4)

The Desert Detectives are thirsty, because the water has run out. But whilst digging they accidentally break a water pipe and get soaked. They catch the water in an old pot. But they suddenly realise the pot is old and might be valuable, so they send it to the Professor. The full script is on page 27.

WORKOUT

Maintain the idea of extreme heat and dryness by having a very slow and gentle workout session today.

THE DESERT DETECTIVES CHALLENGE

Can the Desert Detectives cope without water? Have a race to see who can eat three cream crackers in the shortest time, without a drink. (Be aware of wheat allergies.)

SINGING

You'll know by now which are the children's favourite songs, so make sure you include them. For a change, use songs from previous days in this session, and general songs in the second base camp later on.

THE PROFESSOR/VIDEO

The Professor explains how the kingdom split, and how the various kings disobeyed God, in spite of the prophets' warnings. He focuses in particular on Jeremiah, showing that in the end Jeremiah's warnings came true. The people were invaded by a powerful foreign country and sent away into exile. But God was still looking after his people and he sent other prophets with messages of hope. The full script is on page 42.

The video recaptures in a powerful way how Jeremiah was in a well and how his message was rejected. The Old Testament section of the Bible is completed!

EXPEDITIONS

Beforehand, write out Jeremiah 36:1–7 and 14–25 (or a paraphrase), on a large sheet of paper. Then cut the paper into small pieces and hide them around your room. The children should hunt for the pieces, and put them together to complete the passage.

With a younger expedition, use an enlarged copy of the picture from 5 to 7 year-olds' expedition sheet instead of text.

When the passage or picture is complete, retell or talk about the story.

TENT GROUPS (40 MINUTES)

OASIS

Refreshments

EXPEDITION SHEETS

5 to 7 year-olds look for eight hidden scroll pieces in a picture. Each piece has a letter, and the letters spell 'Jeremiah'.

8 to 11 year-olds use a code to reveal how the king and his servants reacted to the scroll.

Talk about what it means to listen to what God is saying and then to obey him. You could talk about how God wants us to know him and longs to forgive us for the wrong we have done. Make sure that you have enough Bibles or copies of the Bible verses for the older children to engage with the Bible.

CRAFT IDEAS

CRAFT 1: MUSEUM ARTEFACTS

Ideas could include: pottery; scrolls (made from strips of paper and dowelling rods).

CRAFT 2: BIBLE BOOKCASE

Start on the Prophecy books. There are lots of them, but there should be time to finish them tomorrow.

CRAFT 3: FRIEZE PICTURES

Each tent could choose one of the following to make into a picture: Jeremiah at the potter's house; Jeremiah smashing the pot; the king burning the scroll; Jeremiah in the well.

BASE CAMP (20 MINUTES)

SINGING

Sing the **Desert Detectives** song, and some general songs.

MEMORY VERSE

Recap the whole memory verse from John 1:14. See page 47.

POSTBOX

TENT GROUPS (10 MINUTES)

The children return to their tents to finish off their expedition sheets or crafts until they are collected.

HAVE YOU THOUGHT ABOUT...?
WORKING WITH CHILDREN WITH SPECIAL NEEDS

- Always get as much information as possible about the children's needs before you start.

- Designate people to work one-to-one, including working with children with challenging behaviour. As far as possible keep children with disabilities with their own peer group.

- Introduce a code of conduct to the children on the first day. It helps to set boundaries on acceptable behaviour and saves problems later.

- Prepare with a range of abilities in mind – think about wording and abstract ideas. Brief support workers so they know the key theme for each day.

- Have a range of craft ideas available. You might use one from a different age group, but make sure the pictures or other aids are age appropriate.

- Think about the suitability of games you are going to play to ensure the involvement of children with disabilities.

- If you have any child with a hearing loss, make sure they sit near the front and that leaders have their face clearly on view. If the loop system is available, check that it is working for this child. Discussions in small groups can be hard for deaf children. Try to reduce background noise.

- Support workers must be aware of any medical needs which should be requested on the signed registration form. Pay special attention to the use of any medication. (See page 13.)

- Have a registered first-aider on site at all times and keep an accurate accident book.

- Do a risk assessment so that you are aware of any difficulties which might arise.

DAY 4 PROPHECY

Jeremiah wrote God's messages on a scroll and gave it to the king. Use the code to find out what was in the message. Read Jeremiah 36:2,3 to check your answer.

God said to Jeremiah

Get a scroll and write the dreadful

every thing I have told you.

If the people turn to me,

I will forgive them.

Codebreaker

n=⌄⌄   e=ᗰ   i=▲▲▲   o=ᗰ   s=◣◢   t=♕   u=▬▬

FACTFILE

• Prophets of God heard God's message and passed it on.

• They had different jobs. For example, Amos was a shepherd. Jeremiah and Ezekiel were priests. Isaiah worked in the royal palace. Daniel advised a foreign king

---

Find out what happened when the king heard the scroll read out. Read Jeremiah 36:20-25.

Cross out every other letter.

Think hard! Talk with your tent group about the things we do that displease God. Talk about how much God wants us to say sorry and how God wants to forgive us.

Ask God to help you to listen to him and obey him. Thank God that he will forgive us if we ask him to.

Talk with God

BIBLE BOOKCASE

- Fill in the missing books
- Colour these books green.
- Cut them out.

- Stick them into the Prophecy section of your Bible bookcase.

ISAIAH   LAMENTATIONS   EZEKIEL

JOEL   OBADIAH   MICAH   NAHUM   HABAKKUK   ZEPHANIAH   MALACHI

DAY 4 PROPHECY

The king is cutting up Jeremiah's scroll and burning it. Can you find the eight hidden letters? What do they spell? _ _ _ _ _ _ _ _   Colour the picture.

The king would not listen to Jeremiah's message from God. He was not sorry for the wrong things he had done. Read Jeremiah 36:20-26 together.

Think hard! Talk about the things we do that displease God. God wants us to say sorry. Talk about how God wants to forgive us.

Thank God that he will forgive us if we ask him to.

Talk with God

BIBLE BOOKCASE

– Colour these books green.
– Cut them out.

– Stick them into the Prophecy section of your Bible bookcase.

ISAIAH | JEREMIAH | LAMENTATIONS | EZEKIEL | DANIEL | HOSEA | JOEL | AMOS | OBADIAH | JONAH | MICAH | NAHUM | HABAKKUK | ZEPHANIAH | HAGGAI | ZECHARIAH | MALACHI

DAY 5 – GOSPELS

AIMS FOR TODAY

1 To learn that the Bible is the Mighty God's Word

2 To understand that Jesus is God's living Word

3 To understand the significance of Jesus' death and resurrection

4 To respond to Jesus appropriately

LEADERS' PREPARATION

Today is the climax of **Desert Detectives**, because today the Mighty GodSword is finally revealed. But it isn't a sword at all. What the Desert Detectives thought was the Mighty GodSword is really the Mighty God's Word – the Bible. The treasure the Desert Detectives have been looking for is actually what they've been using all week, as they have heard the Bible stories and completed their Expedition sheets.

Read Hebrews 4:12 together and talk and think together about how the Word of God is alive and active, sharper than a two-edged sword. You're not just teaching children old stories. You are giving them the living and active word of God!

But even that's not the whole story, because the Word became human and lived among us (John 1:14). The Bible tells us God's plans for the world, but Jesus shows us.

Use John 1:14 as the basis of your prayers as you prepare today. This is the first day to focus upon Jesus. Children will vary in what they know and understand about him.

TENT GROUPS (10 MINUTES)

As usual, the children begin in their tent groups. This would be a good time to recap the story so far.

BASE CAMP (40 MINUTES)

SINGING

Sing the **Desert Detectives** song and some of the children's favourites from the week.

DRAMA (EPISODE 5)

After a false alarm with a suspected bomb, the Desert Detectives find a gravecloth. If you are not using the video, they will also find a big Bible. They send them to the Professor, unsure what it contributes to their search. They don't know the book is a Bible until the Professor tells them later on. The drama today includes the workout. The full script is on page 29.

WORKOUT

This is included in the drama today.

THE PROFESSOR/VIDEO

The Professor receives the cloth which is identified as a piece of gravecloth, possibly from the tomb of Jesus. The story of Jesus' life, death and resurrection is unpacked. In the script he also receives the Bible. Then the Professor finds both John 1:14 and Hebrews 4:12. He talks about the Bible as God's living word, the Mighty God's Word and then about Jesus, God's living Word. The full script is on page 43.

In the video it is the Professor who first realises that Jesus is the Mighty God's Word. The scene of the crucifixion and resurrection is imaginatively recreated.

THE DESERT DETECTIVES CHALLENGE

Beforehand, write out the first part of Hebrews 4:12 with each word on a separate piece of card. Make one set for each group of participants and attach each set randomly to a large board with blu-tack. The challenge is to see which group can put the words into the right order in the fastest time. During the challenge, play lively music as usual, or sing a song about God's word. 'Father, your word' (kidsource 58) is particularly suitable, but it isn't very long so you would need to sing it several times.

EXPEDITIONS

Divide the expedition into two teams, and have a quiz about Jesus' life and ministry. Ask each team a question in turn. Include questions based on the Professor's summary or the video. But you can also include questions about other well-known stories of Jesus that the children might know. (Remember, you may have some children who know a lot about Jesus and some who know very little. Make sure the latter group of children are not made to feel left out.)

You could include a random scoring element to make it more exciting. For example, when a team gets a question right, ask them to choose a Bible book. The points they get will be equal to the number of chapters in the Bible book they choose. So the points for a question could range from 1 (Philemon) to 150 (Psalms)!

Here are some possible questions.

1 Where was Jesus born?

2 Who came to visit baby Jesus?

3 Who baptised Jesus?

4 Name a miracle Jesus did.

5 Name another miracle.

6 Tell me about a story Jesus told.

7 Tell me another.

8 Tell me about somebody Jesus made well.

9 Think of someone else Jesus healed?

10 Can you think of somebody Jesus brought back to life?

11 Name one of Jesus' special friends. (Older groups should name two)

12 Can you name another one (two)?

13 How did Jesus ride into Jerusalem?

14 What did the crowd do?

15 How did Jesus die?

16 What happened after that?

TENT GROUPS (40 MINUTES)

OASIS

Refreshments

CRAFT IDEAS

CRAFT 1: MUSEUM ARTEFACTS

Ideas could include: gold; frankincense; myrrh; manger; fish and nets; palm leaves; whip (made from rope); last supper items; 30 pieces of silver; Roman soldiers' uniforms; empty tomb model; anything else the children think of from Jesus' parables or ministry!

CRAFT 2: BIBLE BOOKCASE

There are only four books today; the Gospels. But children may also need to finish the Prophecy books from yesterday. If you are not having a service to finish off **Desert Detectives**, you'll need to make sure the children have enough materials to make the rest of the New Testament books at home.

CRAFT 3: FRIEZE PICTURES

Each tent could choose one of the following to make into a picture: the Nativity; the last supper; the crucifixion; the empty tomb; anything else the children think of from Jesus' parables or ministry!

EXPEDITION SHEETS

Both age groups start by considering who the Mighty God's Word is. Younger children may need it to be explained again.

5 to 7 year-olds colour in the shapes with a dot to reveal the word 'Jesus'.

8 to 11 year-olds use the letters from 'Jesus' to complete the memory verse.

Talk about the memory verse (John 1:14) and what it means that God came to live here with us. Share personal experiences of a relationship with Jesus. Explore how Jesus wants us to know and follow him. Invite children who want to know more to talk with you or with one of the other leaders afterwards.

BASE CAMP (20 MINUTES)

SINGING

Sing the **Desert Detectives** song again, but this time change the words to 'Mighty God's Word' instead of 'Mighty GodSword'.

MEMORY VERSE

Recap the whole memory verse from John 1:14 and talk about what it means. Invite a team member to talk about how they began to know and follow the Mighty God's Word.

POSTBOX

If the postbox is full, save some items for the Sunday service.

TENT GROUPS (10 MINUTES)

As this is the last day, tent leaders should make sure the children have all their crafts and expedition sheets to take home. You will want to encourage children to read the Bible for themselves. Details of Scripture Union's Bible-reading resources are on the inside front cover.

Join in Jump on has six titles in the series. This is 50 days of undated material for 5 to 7 year-olds. Some adult input may be necessary.

Snapshots is dated quarterly material for 8 to 10 year-olds, which helps a child to read a few verses of the Bible for themselves, hear from God and talk with him.

HAVE YOU THOUGHT ABOUT...?
PRAYING WITH CHILDREN

When praying with children in a larger group or all together, take care to use simple, clear modern English, free from jargon, keeping it brief and relevant. At the end of the session it would be appropriate to thank God for the time you have had together, the friendships made and the things learnt. As the week progresses you may want to pray all together about things that bother the children or that are in the news. Talking with God should be very natural and the children need to realise this. Explain that we say 'Amen' as a means of saying we agree. We don't have to close our eyes and put our hands together!

Desert Detectives may ask for prayer individually or desire to respond to God by praying by themselves. Pray with a child in the main hall where you can be seen, ideally in a designated quiet area. If their request comes at an inconvenient time, make sure you find time to be with the child later, or pass them on to a leader who is free.

A child may want to make a commitment to Jesus, maybe for the first or tenth time! Ask the child if they have any questions and talk about the important step they are about to make. Explain clearly and simply what it means to follow Jesus. Pray with them a simple prayer, pausing to allow them to repeat each phrase out loud.

Assure the child that God hears us when we pray to him and has promised to forgive us and help us to be his friends if we really want to. You may wish to photocopy a prayer on to a piece of card, with space for the child's name and the date. Encourage them to show it to their parent or carer when they get home, if that is appropriate. Make sure they know about all the other activities that the church runs for children in their age group. *Would you like to know Jesus?* and *Want to be in God's family?* (both SU) will help to explain what it means to follow Jesus. Details are on the inside front cover.

DAY 5 THE GOSPELS

The Mighty God's Word is a person! Write his name here. _ _ _ _ _

Use the letters from his name to complete the memory verse. You can use a letter more than once.

Th_ Word b_cam_ a h_man b_ing and liv_d h_r_ with __. W_ _aw hi_ tr__ glory, th_ glory of th_ only _on of th_ Fath_r. From him all th_ kindn___, and all th_ tr_th of God hav_ com_ down to __. _ohn 1:14

Here are the clues to 14 words in the word search. Think about **Desert Detectives** and you will know all the answers.

The city where Solomon and Jeremiah lived and Jesus died

_____

Where Moses heard the law

_____

The people who blew trumpets around Jericho _____
The walls of Jericho fell down with a _____
The wisest king _____
He was put down a well

_____

Baruch wrote on this _____
Where Jesus was buried _____
The Mighty God_____
The fourth type of Bible book was given by men known as a

_____

J	E	R	U	S	A	L	E	M
E	L	P	L	O	I	D	H	O
R	E	R	R	L	R	N	S	D
E	P	I	B	O	O	X	A	S
M	S	E	W	M	P	R	R	I
I	O	S	A	O	O	H	C	W
A	G	T	L	N	X	T	E	S
H	I	S	T	O	R	Y	X	T

Four types of Bible books:

L _____

H _____

W _____

G _____

Think hard! Talk about the memory verse. What can you remember about how Jesus came to live on this earth with us? And what can you remember about his death and how he came alive again?

Jesus is still alive today. Finish off this prayer. *Thank you Jesus that you are alive today and will be with me after **Desert Detectives**. Thank you that you will be with me at school, at _____, at _____, when I feel _____ and when I am _____ Amen.*

Talk with God

BIBLE BOOKCASE

– Fill in the missing books.
– Colour these books blue.
– Cut them out.
– Stick them into the Gospels section of your Bible bookcase.

MATTHEW MARK LUKE JOHN

Gospels

DAY 5 THE GOSPELS

The Mighty God's Word is a person! Colour in all the shapes with a dot to find his name.

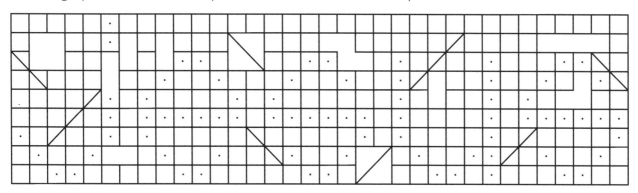

Here are some pictures of Jesus. Put them in the order they happened, then colour them. Write number 1 in the circle in the first picture, and so on.

Talk about the memory verse in John 1:14. Use these pictures to talk about Jesus.

Talk with God

Finish off this prayer

Thank you Jesus that you are alive today and will be with me after **Desert Detectives***. Thank you that you will be with me at school, at* _____, *at* _____, *when I feel* _____ *and when I am* _____ *Amen.*

BIBLE BOOKCASE

– Colour these books blue.
– Cut them out.
– Stick them into the Gospels section of your Bible bookcase.

MATTHEW MARK LUKE JOHN

SUNDAY 2 ACTS-REVELATION

This programme could be adapted to be the seventh day of a holiday club. Alternatively, it is a means of drawing the holiday club to a close, involving parents and friends and making it clear what is planned in the future for children and their families. You may wish to continue the atmosphere of the previous week by holding the service in the **Desert Detectives** venue. Or you may wish to introduce children to a more normal Sunday setting by holding the service in church.

MUSEUM EXHIBITION

If you have been working towards this, lay out the museum artefacts to show how the Desert Detectives have discovered the different books in the Bible and the full Bible story. Select the best craft creations!

INTRODUCTION

Talk about **Desert Detectives** and what has happened during the week. If possible, involve some of the children in this. You could show some of the museum exhibits.

POSTBOX

Show the most interesting items from the week.

THE DESERT DETECTIVES CHALLENGE

Repeat the challenge from Day 5, but use adult volunteers.

MEMORY VERSE

Recap the whole memory verse from John 1:14 and talk about what it means.

PRAYER

Thank God for all that he has done at **Desert Detectives**.

SINGING

Sing the **Desert Detectives** song and other songs. Include songs about Jesus to tie-in with Day 5.

DRAMA (EPISODE 6)

The Desert Detectives begin to fill in their hole. As they do so, they find some parchment that they hadn't spotted before. This turns out to be part of a letter. The full script is on page 31.

THE PROFESSOR/SERMON

Look at the events in the book of Acts, making reference to the letter too. You can use the Professor's script on page 45, or adapt it to use in the sermon. This is the opportunity to complete the review of different types of Bible writing – the letters.

INTERVIEW

Invite a tent leader to talk about their own relationship with Jesus and the importance that the Bible is to them.

SINGING

Sing songs familiar to the children from the week.

PRAYER

Thank God for giving us the Holy Spirit, so that his living Word can be with us always.

REFRESHMENTS AND BOOKSTALL

Children can show their families the museum exhibition and church members can mix with visitors. Have a bookstall with a wide range of Bible-based books and resources.

Other ways to use Desert Detectives

FOLLOW UP FOR CHILDREN AND FAMILIES

Desert Detectives needn't finish when your holiday club does. Why not have a midweek **Desert Detectives** club, or one on a Saturday morning? Or you could use **Desert Detectives** to provide a framework for the teaching in your existing children's activities.

The **Desert Detectives** theme can be used to introduce almost any Bible story. All you have to do is 'discover' an artefact relating to the story you wish to cover. You could also use a particular type of writing as the basis for an extended series. For example, a series based on the Law section could focus each week on a different event in Moses' life, finding a bullrush, or a locust, or a quail's egg. Your imagination is the limit.

Even if you don't carry on with **Desert Detectives** on a regular basis, keep in touch with the children and families you have met through your holiday club. You could have the occasional special service, or a **Desert Detectives** reunion event in one of the school holidays.

USING DESERT DETECTIVES TO TEACH ADULTS ABOUT THE BIBLE

Indirectly, **Desert Detectives** will teach adults about the Bible as they attend the **Desert Detectives** Sunday services, and hear about the week. But you could use it directly too. For example, you could have a special event to trace the Bible story from Genesis right through to Revelation, using the Professor's scripts as an outline. Or you could have a series of evenings, focussing on each of the types of writing. Alternatively, you could use the material as a framework for a Sunday morning teaching programme.

If you made a large Bible bookcase, keep it and refer to it in your church services, to put every Bible reading into its overall biblical context.

ADAPTING THE PROGRAMME FOR THE UNDER-FIVES

POSSIBLE APPROACHES:

- Make parents/carers and toddlers feel welcome when they drop off older children.
- Provide a crèche for the young children of helpers.
- Run a club for younger siblings of club participants and pre-school children.

This will make your holiday club more attractive for families and provide extra avenues for reaching out to parents, carers and younger children. Take each day's theme, simplify it and add pre-school-friendly games, crafts and free play choices. You'll need to think about length of session, facilities available, child/adult ratio and suitable activities.

PARENTS AND TODDLERS

You need a safe, secure space for toddlers to crawl or roam freely with plenty of simple toys. Don't expect to 'lead' activities for more than 10 minutes at a time. Don't worry if children seem oblivious to the theme – the adults will be paying closer attention! Use simple, short and diverse activities – a brief story with a join-in refrain, familiar songs, finger-plays or action rhymes, colouring pictures and creative play tied to the theme. The session need last only an hour.

CRÈCHE

A safe secure space is essential, particularly if there are only one or two adults watching over the children. The crèche session will have to last as long as the holiday club, so you'll need plenty of free play and creative activities, with stories, games and finger-plays for variety. The children will probably include those slightly older than toddlers, so more sophisticated crafts and story-telling are possible.

PRE-SCHOOL CLUB

This could either run for part of the session or last as long as **Desert Detectives**. Children would be nursery school age, possibly integrated into the same space as the holiday club, but with age-appropriate activities, similar to those used in the crèche. Use any appropriate **Desert Detectives** material.

DAY BY DAY

Suggestions for simplified themes related to **Desert Detectives**. Look out for pre-school resources containing suitable stories, finger-plays, songs and action rhymes. Enlarge and photocopy a picture to use each day as a take-home sheet.

DAY 1 – MOSES

      Theme: God gives us laws/doing right
      Story: God told Moses how he wanted people to live (Exodus 19,20)
       Song: Mulberry bush
       Game: Simon Says
Free play: Road mats/cars/traffic rules
       Craft: Chalking on card or pavement
    Picture: Moses holding the tablets

DAY 2 – JOSHUA

      Theme: God is powerful/he helps his people
      Story: The walled city of Jericho was in the way of the people of Israel as they travelled. God's power was So great that he enabled the walls to fall down when his people blew 7 trumpets (Joshua 6)
       Song: The Grand Old Duke of York
       Game: London Bridge is falling down
Free play: Blocks, bricks, and other building toys/noisy musical instruments
       Craft: Toy trumpets, made from coned card
    Picture: The walls of Jericho

DAY 3 – SOLOMON/POETRY

      Theme: Praise God for his goodness
      Story: David wrote many songs to praise God including one about a shepherd (Psalm 23)
       Song: If you're happy and you know it
       Game: Hokey-cokey
Free play: Percussion instruments
       Craft: Make shakers/tambourines
    Picture: David with his harp

DAY 4 – JEREMIAH

      Theme: God wants to make us special to him
      Story: Jeremiah, God's messenger, visited a pottery shop. Just as a potter shapes clay, so God makes us into people who please him (Jeremiah 18)
       Song: The Wheels on the Bus
       Game: One finger, one toe, keep moving
Free play: Play dough
       Craft: Paint a pot
    Picture: A potter's wheel

DAY 5 – JESUS

      Theme: The Good Shepherd
      Story: Jesus told this story. He cares for his sheep as a shepherd and is pleased we're his friends (Luke15)
       Song: Old Macdonald had a farm
       Game: The Farmer's in his den
Free play: Toy farm, animals
       Craft: Make woolly sheep
    Picture: The Good Shepherd

ADAPTING THE PROGRAMME FOR THE OVER-ELEVENS

RUNNING A HOLIDAY CLUB FOR OLDER CHILDREN

THINGS TO THINK ABOUT...

— **Children are maturing earlier** than in previous generations, both physically and emotionally. So ten and eleven-year-olds may not want to be grouped with younger children. How does this affect your planning for **Desert Detectives**?

— **Ages of secondary transfer** vary. Older children in a primary system are likely to accept being in a large all-age group. But children in a middle school system, need to be treated differently. Where do you make the age break for **Desert Detectives**?

— **Approaches to learning** change as a child develops. Children between the ages of 5 and 7 learn by hearing, seeing and doing. Experiencing and articulating feature far more in the learning of a child aged 7 to 10, with reflection becoming more important from 11 onwards. It is hard to cater for these developing styles in one all-age group.

— **The church's work** with 11 to 14 year-olds is vital. This is the time when young people move from a faith position influenced by family to one where peers matter. Does your church have a passion to reach out to young people in this age band?

FEATURES OF A CLUB FOR OLDER CHILDREN

— Enjoyment is important at any age so there needs to be lots of fun!

— Boys are more likely to want energetic involvement while girls may be happier to sit around and talk.

— Young people are more prepared to reflect on issues and ask questions. Discussion is important with everyone's opinion being respected, a more open-ended approach than with younger children.

— Older children want action but of a more sophisticated kind, such as using drama, dance, writing songs and poems, actively listening to music.

— Role models and relationships are important. Recognise this in your planning.

SUGGESTIONS FOR ADAPTING DESERT DETECTIVES

— An older children's programme needs to be separate from the children's programme. Even the title **Desert Detectives** may sound childish. You may want to use a different venue.

— An evening programme may be a better idea. If you run it in the same week as the holiday club (and you have enough people and energy to do so!) ensure the set is suitable to a more relaxed atmosphere.

— Create an informal atmosphere, for example a café scene where non-alcoholic cocktails are served. Call them appropriate names such as 'Sandstorm Surprise'. If you have an upfront presentation, use presenters who are used to working with the age group. And have plenty of time for informal discussion in groups.

— Older children will not tolerate slapstick drama done badly. Adapt the **Desert Detectives** drama but stick to verbal humour if you don't have good actors.

— Music is important. Try to have a good quality live band. Playing CDs in public is against copyright regulations, but you can download MP3 files from the Internet and play those if they are in the public domain.

— The young people could find a series of artefacts which tie in with the theme of the whole Bible story. The audience can work out what they are and how they fit in, depending upon how comfortable with church things they are.

— Interview people who have a story to tell about their faith and what the Bible means to them. Young adults would be especially appropriate.

— *Absolutely Everything* (SU/CPAS) is a series of 11 game-based sessions for 11 to 14 year-olds which explores the whole Bible story. With plenty of ideas and themes to explore in an active way, this may be appropriate for your group.

Whatever you do, run some risks and you will be amazed at how the young people respond.

ORDERING  RESOURCES

To order any of the resources recommended in this book from Mail Order, complete this form.
The books should also be available from a local Christian bookshop.

ISBN	Title	Quantity	Price (each)	Price (each)

When ordering, please include ISBN, title, quantity and price.

All titles subject to availability.

Prices subject to change without notice.

TOTAL COST OF GOODS	
Postage & packing	
Donation to Scripture Union	
Total Enclosed	

ORDERING INFORMATION

Please complete the payment details below.

All orders must be accompanied by the appropriate payment.

Send this completed form to:

Scripture Union Mail Order

PO Box 5148

Milton Keynes MLO, MK2 2YX

Tel: 01908 856006 Fax: 01908 856020

Order Value	UK	Europe	Rest of World	
			Surface	Airmail
£6.00 & under	£1.25	£2.25	£2.25	£3.50
£6.01 – £14.99	£3.00	£3.50	£4.50	£6.00
£15.00 – £29.99	£4.00	£5.50	£7.50	£11.00
£30.00 & over	FREE	PRICE ON REQUEST		

ORDERED BY

Mrs/Mr/Miss/Ms/Rev _____

Address _____

_____

_____

Postcode _____

Daytime tel _____

(for any query about your order)

DELIVERY ADDRESS (if different)

Mrs/Mr/Miss/Ms/Rev _____

Address _____

_____

_____

Postcode _____

Daytime tel _____

(for any query about your order)

PAYMENT DETAILS

Method of Payment ☐ Cheque*   ☐ Mastercard ☐ Visa   ☐ Switch   ☐ Postal order*

Credit card number: ☐☐☐☐ ☐☐☐☐ ☐☐☐☐   Expiry date: ☐☐☐☐

Switch card number: ☐☐☐☐☐☐☐☐☐☐☐☐   Expiry date: ☐☐☐☐

Issue number of switch card: ☐☐☐

Signature: _____   Date: _____

(necessary if payment by credit card)   *made payable to Scripture Union

Please print name which appears on credit card: _____

Please print the address the card is billed to, if different from above: _____

To be included on SU's supporters database and receive our quarterly SU News and other mailings please tick this box ☐ PBHCO1